DEAR TIM

Charles P. De Santo

Introduction by John and Sandra Drescher

DEAR TIM

DEAR TIM

Letters on basic Christian beliefs from
a father to his maturing son.

Charles P. De Santo

Introduction by John and Sandra
Drescher

HERALD PRESS
Scottdale, Pennsylvania
Kitchener, Ontario
1982

Library of Congress Cataloging in Publication Data

De Santo, Charles.
  Dear Tim.

  Summary: A series of letters explaining Christian
beliefs about Christ, God, human nature, the church,
and Christian life.
  1. Theology, Doctrinal—Popular works. 2. Christian
life—1960-   .[1. Theology. 2. Christian life]
I. Title.
BT77.D34   230   81-23744
ISBN 0-8361-1991-6   AACR2

DEAR TIM
Copyright © 1982 by Herald Press, Scottdale, Pa. 15683
    Released simultaneously in Canada by Herald Press,
    Kitchener, Ont. N2G 4M5
Library of Congress Catalog Card Number: 81-23744
International Standard Book Number: 0-8361-1991-6
Printed in the United States of America
Design: Alice B. Shetler

82 83 84 85 86 87 88 10 9 8 7 6 5 4 3 2 1

To Tim
who is what he is by the grace of God in Christ, and
   through interaction with the family—
      his mother and my wife, Norma,
         brother Steve and wife, Nadine,
            sister Debbi and husband, Howard,
               sister Susan and husband, Jack,
                  and niece Erin—
   and kinfolk and friends in the church and the larger
   community

Contents

Introduction

Sandy, I was given a manuscript of a new book by Charles De Santo. The book is in the form of letters to his son Tim who wrote and asked his father to write him letters explaining some of the Christian beliefs and the basis for them. His dad was on a teacher exchange assignment in England at the time. I know you are acquainted with De Santo as the author of the excellent book for young people and parents entitled *Love and Sex Are Not Enough*.

I am intrigued by this new book because all of us know that too often we are not able to carry on convincing and intelligent conversations about what we believe. Further, we may have little understanding of the basis or reasons for these beliefs.

After reading De Santo's letters to Tim I felt that here is an easy-to-understand, down-to-earth, true-to-Scripture course in Christian evidences. Here are statements of foundational beliefs and material to help persons understand the "why" behind these beliefs. I'm wondering what you think about the book. I'd be interested in your response.

✦   ✦   ✦

Thanks, dad, for sharing De Santo's new manuscript with me. As you know, his writing has influenced me in the past and this new book is a continuation of the positive impact.

I was impressed initially with the practical nature from which this book originated. I can relate to Tim's feelings of suddenly finding himself on his own in the world and realizing he doesn't have answers to many of his questions. He knows his dad has found a lot of the answers through his years of experience and knowledge, which he would be glad to share.

Fortunately, as you've often done for me since I left home a few years ago, De Santo meets the challenge of helping to answer Tim's questions. As you also often do, he probably went beyond what was asked of him. I'm sure, however, it was appreciated—both for the interest shown and the insights imparted.

Everyone is not blessed with a prolific parent who can provide permanent documents of belief. For that reason too, I appreciate De Santo's willingness to publish these letters. It would be good to hear some of the specific things you liked in his writing.

✿   ✿   ✿

One of the things I like about the book, Sandy, is that it brings together in simple language much of the material taught at Christian schools and colleges. Mastering what De Santo says about these basic Christian beliefs will provide a good foundation on what it means to be a Christian and a part of the church, on how to study the Bible, and on how to view the Christian faith in relation to other religions.

Also I believe if one learns well what is said here, one will avoid the many wrong concepts thrown our way—not only outright heresies, but distortions by well-meaning persons who seek to prove almost anything by the Scripture. In other words, this book provides an excellent basis for Christian growth and good help for spiritual discernment.

✿   ✿   ✿

I agree, dad. I especially enjoy De Santo's practical way of being both thorough and understandable. Too often, Bible scholars seem to use a language too complicated for the average person. In speaking to Tim as a son, he writes in a personal and informal manner. At the same time, he shares the essential reasons for his beliefs. After reading each letter I get the distinct feeling of having learned something worthwhile without the usual concentration that studying requires.

As you mentioned, I also appreciated his overall view of the Christian faith, as opposed to using specific verses attempting to prove certain doctrines. His emphasis on wanting Tim to test his beliefs with many people rather than following any one influential leader is good. It makes each letter a tried and true set of principles, but encourages additional personal testing.

✿   ✿   ✿

Another thing I enjoyed in the book, Sandy, is the way the author provides what I'd call "think statements"—statements or illustrations which cause the questioner or disbeliever to stop and weigh the evidence. I've found many times that unbelievers, or those who say they have difficulty accepting spiritual truth, actually have given little thought to the subject. Unbelief has managed to come up with no new argument in a thousand years. The old arguments are simply repeated over and over. De Santo, for example, points out that the person who says the crutch of religion is not needed actually has many crutches in social and business and physical life.

In speaking of the Christian church he writes, "Only the Christian church has given her sons and daughters, as well as substance, to minister throughout the world in relief (food and clothing), medical, educational, agricultural, technical, and evangelistic programs."

✿   ✿   ✿

I was thinking about the thoroughness in the Christian faith which offers us a complete meaning in life, too, dad. De Santo's mention of the crutches we use and the fact that everyone needs some sort of help from a more powerful source reminds me of the sensibleness of following Christ. Since God has the most control in this world, serving him is the smartest and most secure thing I can do! His extra benefits of being a God of love and mercy are clinchers that make me wonder why anyone would continue struggling through life alone. I'm increasingly confirmed in this feeling the farther I read through these letters. De Santo deals with every aspect of life and always comes out with God not only having *an* answer, but *the best* answer.

The relevance of faith in Christ (that he begins with) is shown in every letter. Passing these truths on to a son seems to me to be the greatest gift a father could give. Giving this book to a son or daughter will be a tremendous gift, especially handy for those who don't have the time or ability to compile such a concise and complete work themselves.

✿   ✿   ✿

Your comments are helpful, Sandy. I believe *Dear Tim* can provide a foundation for the faith of many young people. Older Christians can also profit from these pages.

These letters provide discussion starters for youth groups and Sunday school classes. They are good resource for a series of sermons to enrich a congregation's understanding of the church's basic beliefs. What additional uses do you see for the book?

✦   ✦   ✦

I can think of several seminary as well as high school and college Bible classes I've had, dad, in which this book would have been a helpful addition to the required readings or a good supplement for further study. It's easy enough to read in a short time but also covers more issues than can be digested in one sitting. Because of that, it's a good reference book to refer to as questions come up. Using the book as a discussion starter in sermons or small groups is a way to find and own these truths. To refer back to the book for a refresher and for additional insight could also prove valuable.

I hope many persons of all ages will find these letters written personally for them, either in deciding for the first time that the Christian faith is the one they want to follow or as further encouragement along the path already chosen.

John M. Drescher and daughter, *Sandra,* authors of book, *When You Think You Are in Love,* an exchange of a year's letters between daughter and father (Abbey Press).

Author's Preface

My wife, Norma, and I have been blessed with four fine children—each unique in his/her own way. (Unbiased reporting, of course!) Each one of them—Steve, Debbi, Susan, and Tim—has enriched our lives beyond measure. (For one thing, they've taught us what to do, and what not to do as parents. It's too bad we didn't know that when they were infants!) Through tough times and good times we have worked things out together. Not everyone was happy at the same time, but in retrospect it has been a great experience.

I think that subconsciously, as well as consciously, the one who has held us together and given us a sense of direction has been our Lord Jesus Christ. What we tried to give our children, more than anything else, was a faith to live by—the Christian faith. But we weren't the only ones who shared Christ with them. Norma and I are indebted to our parents and relatives who helped nurture us and them, as we are to a host of Christian friends in the churches in which we have fellowshiped over the years.

We're especially thankful to God that all of our children have embraced Christ and committed their lives to him. Tim, the youngest of the brood, has followed brother Steve and sisters Debbi and Susan in this commitment—for which we are grateful.

In 1978 we had the opportunity to return to England where I served as an exchange professor of sociology at Trent Polytechnic at Nottingham. The entire family had been there the academic year of 1972-73. At that time Tim was about to turn thirteen. During his first year in England Tim attended Fairham Comprehensive High School where he became seriously involved in sports—gymnastics, trampoline, kayaking (they called it canoeing), and Ping-Pong. Kayaking was his favorite. He went out with the college students on the murky Trent River. He wanted to go with them to the Welsh Coast to kayak in the sea; fortunately the weather turned bad and they called off the trip!

After we returned home in August of 1973, Tim became interested in motorcycles. For a few dollars, his older brother, Steve, bought Tim a small cycle, which he rode around the yard. Tim soon outgrew that small bike. But the summer after he turned fifteen, he worked as a dishwasher at a truck stop on the interstate several miles from home. And what did he do with the money? Most of it went toward buying a trail bike to ride on the hills and racecourse around Mackeyville. We prayed that he'd lose interest. After a year he sold it to buy a kayak. He worked at kayaking for over a year before he sold it. By then his interest in tennis was growing and he went at that with all the enthusiasm he could muster. (If he would only divert some of his energy into his studies.)

Tim went to summer tennis camp and had a few private lessons. He played long and hard—wearing out many pairs of expensive tennis shoes. During the winter of his junior year in high school he discovered skiing! He could use his natural dexterity and his acquired skills in gymnastics at skiing. But Tim wasn't content just to ski; he had to do aerials (somersaults), ski ballet, and the like. At last he had found his niche. Skiing would be his avocation and vocation, Tim decided. Through his senior year in high school and for the past four years he has pursued his career of skiing—hoping to go pro in due time. Given his dedication, discipline, and self-imposed rigorous training schedule, he'll make it!

Tim's senior year in high school was a vast improvement over his first three years. While he didn't make the honor roll, his grades were much better. However, the event that helped turn him around spiritually happened shortly after graduation. His friend Greg experienced a dramatic conversion. Greg, whose many problems included drug abuse, did a complete about-face. The change that Christ produced in Greg's life had a profound influence on Tim. God used Greg's experience to speak to Tim, with the result that Tim renewed his commitment to Christ. From that significant leap forward, Tim has continued to forge ahead.

When Norma and I went to England again in the fall of 1978, Tim headed out west to Sun Valley, Idaho, to work and ski. But after a few months, he returned to Oregon Hill, Pennsylvania, to work and train at the ski resort. While there, Tim wrote with the following request:

> Dad, it would be very helpful to me if you would write me several letters explaining some of our basic Christian beliefs. Also, it would be helpful if you would write something about a Christian lifestyle—relating Christianity to my life in today's world. Also, please share other things that you feel are necessary to know and study as a growing Christian. I'll be waiting for them!

As you can imagine, I was encouraged and pleased with his apparent progress in the faith, and challenged by his request. I answered Tim:

About your request for some letters explaining basic Christian beliefs and giving some hints about Christian behavior, I'll try to do this soon. I'll begin while here at Trent Polytechnic on this teacher exchange, as time permits. They'll probably get to you at irregular intervals, and you can build on them as you read further from the Word of God and from the wide store of Christian literature.

The summer of 1981 I finally finished the series of letters that I began in the fall of 1978. Tim and others have had a chance to read them several times and give me helpful feedback.

While I have addressed these letters to Tim, my youngest son, in reality I'm sharing them with my other children as well—Steve, Debbi, and Susan. I hope the letters will stimulate their thinking about basic Christian beliefs and also serve as a means of Christian growth. I'm glad that many other young people will look over Tim's shoulder and read these letters also. If you have already given your life to the Lord, I hope that the letters will help you grow in your faith. If you have not, I pray that reading the letters with an open mind will nudge you toward embracing Christ as your own Savior and the Lord of your life.

Charles P. De Santo
Nottingham, England, 1978
Mackeyville, Pennsylvania, 1981

The Relevance of
Faith in Christ

Dear Tim,

I thought I'd take this opportunity to say how glad I am that you have deepened your commitment to Christ. The new forward strides you've taken are most gratifying. You and your brother Steve and sisters Debbi and Susan have always taken faith in God seriously. It has been a real joy to see each of you make the initial commitment of your life to Christ and then to go on with him. I'm glad that you've asked me to write a series of letters sharing the basic beliefs of the Christian faith with you. I hope the basic biblical ideas contained in these letters will enlarge and deepen your understanding of the Christian faith, stimulate you to further study, and better equip you in your witness to others. In addition, I hope you'll share these letters with some of your Christian and non-Christian friends.

Tim, one question you'll encounter frequently is this: Is the Christian faith relevant? It's an important question and deserves some serious consideration.

Quite often I meet young people who, for a variety of reasons, are turned off with schooling—high school and college. They'll say, "I just don't think that schooling is relevant." I'm usually jolted by such statements, not just because I'm a college teacher, but because I consider learning as essential to life as food, water, and air. Those who dare to ask serious questions about life and their future—about the contribution they hope to make to themselves, their families, the community, and society at large—have no difficulty seeing the part that learning and education play in life.

When I hear people say, "I just don't think that Christianity is relevant to life today," I'm also shocked. It beats me how they can say that. They must be asking the wrong questions! Or if they're asking the right questions, they're failing to look in the right place for the answers.

Invariably, everyone raises questions such as: Who am I? Why am I here? What is life all about? Is life just fun and games, or is there a purpose behind it all? Are we all made out of the same stuff? Are we all really "brothers and sisters"—all children of the one God? Can I find the way to a useful, meaningful life? Is there a supreme being who is loving *and* just? Did God just create the world and abandon it? Does he really care about us individually? How can I know him? Has he revealed himself? When? Where? How? Questions such as these virtually compel one to look to Christianity, to Christ, and to the Bible for answers.

But why is it that so many people do not turn to Christ? There are a variety of reasons why. For one thing, if a person gets serious about God, then he can't do as he pleases. He has to begin to ask, What does God want me to do with my life? How should I use my talents, time, and possessions? Can I really do this or that? Can I exploit others to achieve my own ends? I remember getting into a discussion with some Christians who owned a business. They felt that they could pay their employees whatever *they* chose to. The idea that they were accountable to God and that they should treat their employees as "family members" was something they had not considered. Of course, the easy way out is just to reject the whole religious lot! But isn't that a cop-out? Isn't that cowardly?

Unfortunately, some people think life has given them a dirty deal. Perhaps their dad or mom seriously disappointed them or abused them in some way. Perhaps they experienced a serious tragedy in their lives. Sometimes their pastor or Christians whom they held in high esteem let them down. (Incidentally, Tim, that's a good reason for putting your faith and trust in Christ and God, not man. After all, each of us is a sinner, and unfortunately we still fall into sin from time to time after we've become Christians.) It's difficult for some to see how God can be loving and just when their family or life-situation has been so harsh. You can understand how they might react—I can. It is difficult to think of God as a loving Father if you've never known one. On the other hand, if one has not had a good parent, the *good news* of the gospel—that God the Father is loving and compassionate—should be welcomed enthusiastically.

Still another reason why people don't turn to God in faith is that they are uninformed. They are biblically and theologically illiterate—some through no fault of their own, but others by choice. Still others are content with a child's knowledge of Christianity. They have not bothered to read the Bible seriously or systematically, let alone read books dealing with the Christian philosophy of life and Christian theology. It seems inconsistent to me that some are willing to live with an immature understanding of the Christian faith, whereas they wouldn't for a moment think of remaining at a child's level in math, science, or other spheres of knowledge. How many do you know who try to operate with an elementary school knowledge of math or science? Not many. Why then do people refuse to explore the faith or reject it without giving it a fair hearing?

You'd be surprised at the number of peculiar ideas people have about God. It's often because of ignorance or bias that is not entirely of their own doing that some pursue bogus religions, secular humanism, various ideologies, and weird cults and sects. Many end up as hedonists, making the pursuit of pleasure their goal in life. Sensuous pleasure—fun and games—becomes the be-all and end-all of existence. When you wrote from the ski resort out west you mentioned that you weren't too happy because a majority of the people there only seemed to be interested in "having fun." They demonstrated little concern for morality or for the needs and welfare of others. While many may have heard of God, they seemed to reject him. My guess is that their knowledge and concept of God bore little resemblance to the God revealed in Christ or Scripture.

Some people, no doubt, reject Jesus because of the "cost factor." Not realizing the joy of the Christian life, they are unwilling to give up the sensual pleasures of our permissive society. Or perhaps they are unwilling to accept the ethical demands of Christ—unwilling to take seriously the notion that we are to be our brother's keeper.

Unfortunately, many persons are caught up in the mad pursuit for material things. *Things* become their master. Conspicuous consumption, like the old consumption (TB—tuberculosis), grabs hold of them. Their life goal is to surround themselves with things that will make them appear superior or better than others. Their goals is not merely to keep up with the Joneses, but to get ahead of them. Accumulating the symbols of the successful life (costly clothes, cars, furniture, and palatial homes) becomes the main motivating factor in life. Unfortunately, many realize too late the truth of Jesus' words, "A man's life does not consist in the abundance of his possessions" (Luke 12:15).

In secular society, money brings power, but power has a tendency to corrupt. This is well demonstrated by the corruption and scandals within political parties, large national and multinational corporations, trade unions, and even within the church. Money, power, and pleasure have a way of becoming gods—idols. When one is worshiping such an idol, it's awfully difficult to see the one true God and worship him. Tim, I really believe that Christianity *is* relevant, but for a variety of reasons people refuse to consider it. In many cases they are blinded by the "god of this world" who prevents them from seeing God's truth (2 Corinthians 4:4; 3:14; 1 Corinthians 8:4-6).

You've probably met people who claim that they have rejected God and religion altogether. But if you scratch beneath the surface and probe a bit, you'll find them quite religious. The difference between you and them is that the paraphernalia and behavior patterns (rituals) of their religion are not traditionally recognized as being "religious." One of my friends began each semester of his course on the Christian faith by saying to his students, "Why don't you get a gun and go blow your brains out?" I can imagine the shocked reaction he got from those first-year college students. What a way to begin a course! He went on to point out that whatever keeps us from doing that and whatever keeps us going is really our religion. Sometimes the religion includes a supreme being, but many times it doesn't.

For some the driving force within them is a political or philosophical ideology like Marxism, communism, or fascism, while for others it might be nationalism. For others the most important thing in life is a veteran's organization, a fraternity, or sorority. Still others replace the church with a civic club, country club, or local tavern. It's amazing how "religious" some irreligious people are about attendance and participation in these religious surrogates or substitutes.

On the intellectual level you'll find professors and other well-educated people who claim to be agnostic or atheistic. What they often fail to acknowledge is that even agnosticism and atheism require a "leap of faith," as Andrew Greeley points out. They too are making assumptions about ultimate reality. An atheist unconsciously claims to be omniscient (knows it all) when he makes the unqualified statement, "God does not exist!" Frankly, Tim, I find the atheistic position completely untenable.

But the biggest snare is relativism. You'll find people who say, "Well, it's all relative anyway. Some people look at it this way, and some look at it that way. It all depends on how you look at it. What is right for you may be right for you, but it's not necessarily right for me." The notion of cultural relativity is widely acknowledged. But few thinking Christians would agree (nor many sociologists and anthropologists) that things are absolutely relative. Many ideas about human nature and behavior are found in all societies. All cultures have ideas about honesty, theft, and fidelity within marriage (regardless of the family structure, whether it's a polygamous or monogamous one). The basic needs of mankind do not vary that much, regardless of the structure of a given society. The significant differences between societies are the ways in which these universals are expressed—the way each society designs rules and behavior patterns to meet its basic needs.

C. S. Lewis makes the point in *Mere Christianity* that the notion of relativity is usually employed when one sees that he can profit by it. But if *you* decided to take the relativist's bicycle, telling him when he objected, "My friend, you may think that it is your bicycle, but now it is mine!" he'd probably punch you in the nose. Truth is truth. Even the so-called relativist admits this when *he* is involved. Much as one might like to cop out by denying God and the fact that there are absolutes, one cannot. The choice is either the freedom that comes by faith in God through Christ, or enslavement to a false "god" (Matthew 11:28-30; John 8:34-36).

Several years ago my sociology class was discussing the place of religion in society. One student spoke up saying, "I don't need God and the church; I don't need a crutch." At first there was a murmur of agreement by some, and then a period of silence. But gradually the students entered into a stimulating give-and-take discussion of religion and religious surrogates. We all discovered that he, and others like him, were not as independent and self-reliant as they had assumed. As it turned out, they belonged to groups, organizations, and fraternities and sororities. They associated with guys and girls who shared their interests and goals. They had a philosophy of life and they associated with people who shared a similar philosophy of life and similar social interests. They were using a crutch! Most of them admitted that man is a social being who needs others. He needs support—friends with similar ideas, friends with whom he can fellowship. Actually, if you think of an ideological system and social needs as a support, instead of a crutch, everyone has one or more that he uses to understand life. It seems to me, Tim, that faith in God revealed in Christ and the Scriptures is the only support that enables one to stand on his own two feet and throw away his crutches (Mark 2:1-12).

Finally, at college or university you'll probably meet some sharp lecturers and professors who will not be Christians. They may seem impeccable in character, keen of intellect, kind, and compassionate. And they probably are. They may appear to have it "all sewed up"—have the world by the tail, so to speak. But remember that all men and women have feet of clay. We can't get into their skin. (Originally I wrote "their sin!" That is probably true, too. For all have a private, secluded life known only to the individual and God.) Inside they have the same questions and struggles that you and I have; it's just that some, for a variety of reasons, *seem* to function all right without God (Proverbs 14:12). But isn't that really the greatest sin of all—when one says to almighty God, who poured out his love in Jesus Christ, "I choose not to recognize your existence. I am not willing to acknowledge you as the source of all life-sustaining graces." Isn't that (pride) the most serious sin (Luke 18:9-14)? And isn't ingratitude just about as bad (Luke 17:11-19; Romans 1:21-32)? Actually, Tim, you'll find that many of the really great intellects have been humble men who have professed faith in God. In fact, many who come to faith in God through Christ, after having once been skeptical and unbelieving, have testified that, by comparison, their previous life was devoid of true meaning (Philippians 3:4-11).

Are Christ and Christianity relevant? Yes indeed! Already you've begun to find it so because you have been brave enough to face the difficult questions—the ultimate ones. In later letters I want to think through with you some of the basic Christian doctrines, interpreting them in a way that I hope will be clear, meaningful, and helpful. As you read the letters I hope you'll respond honestly to what I have said and pursue the ideas further by looking at God's Word and some of the good Christian books that are available.

Take care of yourself. The Lord bless you, Tim.

All my love,
Dad

The Basic Message
of the Bible

Dear Tim,

When you think about Christianity, it's natural to think about Jesus Christ. Usually we learn about God within the context of the family; through various worship, educational, service, and social activities in the church; and through our own personal reading. Most learning, however, occurs through interaction and dialogue with others. This is true of learning about our faith, as well as other areas of thought. But the basic source of information for our faith is the Bible. It is *the book*. The Greek word *biblos* means book. Often you'll hear people refer to a definitive, authoritative book on a particular subject as the "bible" of that subject or activity. For example, you might refer to some work as the "bible for skiers," a sport to which you're dedicated and have professional aspirations.

While your faith is in God and Christ, not in a book, the Bible authentically preserves the record of God's revelation. If you want to know anything about the Christian faith, the Bible is the one reliable source. This is not to say that God has not revealed himself apart from, or outside of, Scripture. He has. But if you want to know what he has to say to you about who man is, what one ought to believe, and how one ought to behave, the Bible is the place to look.

Some well-intentioned persons attempt to make the Bible an authority for science, psychology, sociology, history, and the like. This only leads to confusion and conflict. The Bible was never intended to be the compendium of secular knowledge and thought. It is a religious book, the revelation of God to mankind (2 Timothy 3:16-17). Although archaeologists have confirmed the historical accuracy of the biblical narrative, and the psychological and sociological insights into individual and group behavior are trustworthy, the Bible is not a text in those fields. It is a religious book. God speaks to us through his dealings with the nation of Israel, through the life and teachings of Jesus, and through the literature of the early church preserved in the letters and writings of the New Testament (Hebrews 4:12; Psalm 119:105; John 14:26; Ephesians 6:17). Let me share several more things about the Bible with you in more detail, Tim.

For one thing, the Bible is a record of God's revelation to us through his dealings with Israel, the Jews (Hebrews), and finally through our Lord Jesus Christ (Hebrews 1:1-3). On the one hand, the Old Testament contains the history of Israel, together with the writings of the prophets and other historical, poetical, and literary writings. It looks forward to the coming of the Messiah. On the other hand, the New Testament records the fact that the Messiah has come. It contains the record of God's revelation in the life and teachings of Jesus Christ, the Messiah, as well as the interpretation and application of his life and teachings to the church.

We actually need both testaments to understand the Christian faith. The Old Testament begins with the origin of things, including mankind. Then it tells of the call of Abraham (the "father" of the Hebrew people), the establishment of the nation Israel under Moses (through the Exodus and the covenant at Mt. Sinai), and its rise and subsequent fall as a nation. The Old Testament doesn't whitewash Jewish history. It tells of the disobedience and corruption of the Jewish people, as well as their obedience to God and the example they set for other nations. The prophets figure largely in the Old Testament, as they call the various Jewish institutional leaders and the lay people to repent and renew their faith in God.

Gradually, what you see emerging in the Old Testament is the messianic hope, the hope that God will intervene by sending his Messiah. When the Jews, the people of God, failed to respond to the prophetic call to repentance, the prophets proclaimed the coming of God's judgment. Incidentally, the prophets were not "fortune-tellers," as some would have us believe. They were "proclaimers of the Word of God" to the people of their day. When they did predict the future, it was usually connected with the immediate and long-range consequences of the people's obedience or disobedience to God. In addition to the prophets' words of judgment they also uttered words of hope and promise— that God would some day send the Messiah, an anointed deliverer. Taking the Old Testament as a whole, the Messiah is presented as embodying the roles of prophet, priest, and king. We'll talk more about Jesus Christ later.

The New Testament contains the fulfillment of this prophetic hope. The four Gospels (the word gospel means "good news") give an authentic record of the life and teachings of Jesus Christ (*Christ* is the Greek word for Messiah, the "anointed one"). The best manuscripts of the New Testament books go back to within a hundred years of the actual composition of most of the New Testament writings. This is better than we have for most ancient writings.

The Gospels, strictly speaking, do not contain the complete record of Christ's life—his teachings and works. The book would be unmanageably large (John 21:25). They do give us, however, the essential facts of his life and ministry. These books were written by his followers, persons who were either his disciples and apostles, or believers who associated with those who knew Jesus personally. Their own lives had changed dramatically because of him.

Sometimes, Tim, you'll run across people who claim that the gospels can't be reliable because they were written by believers. The implication is that believers would distort the facts to make Jesus Christ divine. My answer is that only a believer could really know Jesus Christ and give an authentic picture of him (John 20:24-29; Acts 9:1-20; 2 Corinthians 5:16). You and I have both had the experience of having someone speak disparagingly of a friend. You remember the time when someone said some nasty things about Kevin. You said that you knew Kevin, and that what they said could not be true. As it turned out, you were right! So the gospels were written by men of faith, and rightly so. For only those who shared the joys and sorrows of Jesus' ministry really understood him. Only persons of faith could write authentically to bring us to faith (Luke 1:1-4; John 20:31; Acts 1:1-2).

The Acts of the Apostles, the fifth book of the New Testament, gives us a reliable account of the *proclamation* of the apostles (called the *kerygma*) and their teachings (called *didache*). It tells of the birth and growth of the early church. The epistles (letters) of the New Testament all fit into that history, containing not only theological teachings as a basis for faith, but also messages to members and leaders within the churches about Christian behavior. Once again, Tim, you'll notice the New Testament writings *do not* whitewash conditions within the early church. The same problems we face in the church today—conflict, jealousy, disobedience, immorality, partiality (prejudice and discrimination), coldness, and the like—were all present then (1 Corinthians 3:1-4; 5:1). In fact, the reason the apostles wrote to churches and to individuals was to challenge them to put things in order, to encourage them to act like Christians—to love each other, and to reach out to serve in the name of Christ. They were not merely writing theological or ethical treatises.

The last book in the New Testament, Revelation, is a unique one, as you well know. It is different from all the other New Testament books. It is highly symbolic. Technically, it is classed as *apocalyptic literature*. Apocalypse means "to reveal or to unveil." The author uses symbols to paint pictures to convey his message. The basic message of an apocalypse is that God will deliver his people from the "bad times" they are now undergoing. In the apocalypse of John, the book of Revelation, the author offers hope to those suffering under oppressive Roman emperors. Martin Luther and John Calvin recognized the highly symbolic and complex nature of the book and urged Christians not to be preoccupied with it. Frankly, Tim, as one who specialized in the study of Old and New Testament apocalyptic literature, I would agree. Concentrate on the 90 percent of the Scriptures that is comparatively easy to understand—whose message is unmistakably clear.

With this overview of the Bible, brief and inadequate as it may be, let me share some things that I think will be helpful as you read and study the Bible. I recommend that you read from a modern translation such as *Good News Bible, The New English Bible, The New International Version,* or the *Revised Standard Version.* Of course, the best translation or version is the one we actually get busy and read.

Before I close this letter, let me say a word about the Bible's relevance for us today. You'll meet people who say, "The Bible is an ancient book. How can it speak to us today? World conditions, our type of government, theories about the cosmos, and the like, are all so different today. It can't possibly address itself to those of us living in modern societies." On the surface it might appear they have a point. I *used* to think they did. But "the more things change, the more they stay the same." Or as the writer of Ecclesiastes said, "There's nothing new under the sun!"

It's true, our modern technological developments have been mind bogglingly rapid and complex. The world we live in is vastly different from the world I lived in as a boy, not to mention the world of Jesus' day. But (and there is a *but*) man's essential nature and needs have not changed. Western dress, motorized transportation, nuclear weapons, all of modern science and social science *have not* altered the nature of man *nor* rectified the perennial problems that plague individuals, families, groups, and nations. The timeless Word of God is just as incisive, dynamic, and life-giving as it was when first spoken (Deuteronomy 8:3; Isaiah 55:11; Matthew 24:35; John 6:63, 68; Hebrews 4:12; 1 Peter 1:23-25). The Word is still relevant because God's spirit works through it to speak to us. In a sense there is no "new Word" of God to us, for the "old" revelation of God to us is forever "new."

Brian Haymes, pastor of the Mansfield Road Baptist Church here in Nottingham, emphasized in his sermon last Sunday the eternal relevance of God's Word. He recalled what the prophet Jeremiah said to Zedekiah, king of Judah, who asked him if he had a "new word" from the Lord. "No, oh king, it's the same 'old word'—the one I gave you earlier which you have not been willing to receive" (Jeremiah

37:16-17). And I would add the words of John: "My dear friends, this commandment I write to you is not new; it is the old command, the one you have heard from the very beginning . . . we must love one another" (2 John 5; 1 John 2:7; 3:11; John 13:34; Leviticus 19:18).

So the Word is relevant, Tim. So long as man *is*, the Word speaks to us. Unlike "ordinary truths" which become obsolete and irrelevant, the truth of God's Word never does (Psalm 119:89; Matthew 5:18; Isaiah 55:11). If we ignore it, if we fail to learn God's truth and keep it within our hearts and minds, then we are likely to fall for anything (Psalm 119:11; Jeremiah 2:13). (Think of the tragedy in Guyana where over 900 members of the People's Temple commune committed mass suicide.) But if we nurture ourselves on it, then we'll have a basis of comparison when we encounter error (Acts 17:11).

Just one other thing, Tim. You'll notice a recurring theme running through the experience of the people of God in both the Old and New Testaments. The people sin, they are called to repentance, they confess their sin, God forgives them, they are reconciled to God and to those whom they have offended, and their religious experience is renewed (2 Chronicles 7:14; Psalm 32:1-5; 51; Luke 11:4; 1 John 1:9). The process is still going on today. We hope as we go on with Christ we'll fall into sin less often. But when we do sin, remember the call of the prophets, Jesus, and the apostles to return to the God who longs to receive us back and renew the estranged relationship.

So then, Tim, the Bible *is* the Word of God—authoritative, completely trustworthy, and wholly reliable. The Old Testament contains the revelation of God, his will and purposes for Israel and all mankind. Out of the historical experience of the Hebrews the prophets predicted the coming of the Messiah. The New Testament shows how this hope was realized or fulfilled in Jesus Christ our Lord. In addition, it tells how the apostles and the early church not only embraced the good news, but also shared it with both Jews and Gentiles. By the work of God in Christ those who believe are saved and made members of Christ's body, the church. In Christ all divisions between peoples are broken down (Galatians 3:26-28; Ephesians 2:13-16).

Remember, Tim, that while the Word of God was revealed to holy men of God over several centuries, the Holy Spirit blended it all into a beautiful cohesive document of God's redeeming love. Because it is God's Word to mankind, it is timeless. Mankind's basic needs do not change. Therefore, for us as Christians the Bible becomes our basic frame of reference from which we take our cues for behavior, as well as the standard by which we judge all other philosophies, doctrines, and practices.

I'll close now. I've written more than I intended to. In my next letter I'll share some principles of interpretation with you. Until then, Tim, God bless you through his Word. Take care.

All my love,
Dad

Principles for Understanding God's Word

Dear Tim,

In my last letter I shared with you some truths about the message of the Bible. Now let me set forth some principles of interpretation that will be helpful as you read and study the Bible.

First, the Bible is a book that requires a great deal of study to accurately interpret it. Fortunately, those with only basic reading ability can receive comfort, guidance, and strength from it. But to receive the most from it, you must give it a lot of time and serious study. Martin Luther felt strongly about this. He said we ought not to think that we can interpret the Bible properly until we've studied it for 500 years. (But then he wrote volumes about it during his short lifetime.) Tim, the point is that you can draw upon a wealth of Bible study aids—commentaries, dictionaries, and the like—to help you maximize your understanding. The Holy Spirit, who works through the Word to teach us about God and his will for us, can be more effective if we stock our minds with knowledge about biblical times, conditions, and various interpretations (John 16:13). God doesn't help us remember and apply things from His word that we have never learned.

You do have to be careful, though. On the one hand there is a segment of biblical scholarship that is academic, but highly critical, skeptical, and destructive. Some people write so-called scholarly books, but their aim seems to be to tear down and destroy faith, rather than build it up. There's little to be gained from reading them. On the other hand, there are those who attempt to imitate God by creating doctrines "out of nothing." Often they misinterpret Scripture and, as Jesus said about the Pharisees, when they get through with an individual they make him twofold times more a child of hell than he was before (Matthew 23:15). So choose wisely, read widely, but always evaluate everything in the light of Christ's teachings in Scripture. There are enough good evangelical scholars around to keep you busy for Luther's 500 years.

Second, keep in mind that the Bible is a historical book. God revealed himself through history, and the revelation of himself culminates in Jesus (Galatians 4:4-5; Hebrews 1:1-3). Jehovah's Witnesses and many unschooled Christians, as well as numerous sects, ignore the historical approach to Bible study. By their interpretation, the prophets delivered messages to people in their time that were totally irrelevant to their condition. As I mentioned earlier, the prophets were spokesmen for God who preached a message of judgment and hope primarily for their day, and only secondarily for some future day. If you know the history of the times, their message makes good sense, and you can easily apply the message and meaning to our present personal and historical setting. But if you ignore the historical context of the prophetic message, then you are apt to accept all sorts of unfounded and false interpretations. Furthermore, those interpretations are subject to revision with every change on the political scene. People like that tend to become preoccupied with predicting the end of the world and neglect functioning as God's agents for change in this world. I'm not denying the future hope of prophecy in the Old Testament, but when you're dealing with the end-time it's best to be cautious. Even Jesus said that he didn't know when the end would come, and he was closer to God than Preacher Know-it-all (Mark 13:32). Jesus' preoccupation was to do the will of God now, here in this life (John 4:34; Mark 10:45). We would do well to witness to the salvation he offers in this life and serve him here and now. God will take care of the end time.

Third, it might be helpful if I shared something about the kinds of narrative and literary forms found in the Bible. First of all, you'll notice a variety of types of writing within the Bible: prose narrative, poetry, parables, allegories, metaphors, similes, and apocalyptic. Apocalyptic writers like John (the one who wrote Revelation), for example, use word symbols to paint pictures to convey their message. Therefore, you don't take it literally, although you do take it seriously. You attempt to draw out its main message. For example, 1 Thessalonians 4:16-17 reads, "For the Lord himself shall descend from heaven with a shout, with the voice of the archangel, and with the trump of God: and the dead in Christ shall rise first: then we which are alive and remain shall be caught up together with them in the clouds, to meet the Lord in the air: and so shall we ever be with the Lord." Here the main idea is that Christ will come in triumph and Christians who are dead, as well as Christians who are alive at his appearing, will share in the blessings of the eternal kingdom. If you took it literally and pressed details, you would walk about with your head pressed back against your spine and your ear cocked, listening for the "shout, the voice, and the trumpet."

Likewise, metaphors such as Christ's words, "I am the

door," "I am the vine," and "I am the bread of life," are figures of speech that express real truths about our Lord (John 10:9; 15:5; 6:35). Robert Frost, the great American poet, said that "a person without training in metaphor is not safe anywhere." I would agree. Jesus is the door into the kingdom, he is the vine from which we draw spiritual sustenance, and he is the bread that nourishes our souls. In allegories such as the vine and the branches, each phrase or item has a symbolic meaning. Parables, on the other hand, have one main meaning. In the parable of the sower or soils, the main point is that only those who persevere, only those who receive the Word (the gospel) and continue in the faith, bearing fruit, will be saved (Mark 4:1-20).

Poetry, unlike prose, conveys ideas through word pictures. When the psalmist says that the righteous person "is like a tree planted by streams of water, that yields its fruit in season" (Psalm 1:3), he obviously is using an analogy to convey how the obedient believer is blessed of God. Likewise, when Isaiah speaks of the future deliverance and restoration of Israel he says that "all the trees of the field will clap their hands" (55:12). The main idea is that it will be a time of joy and rejoicing.

Especially approach with caution passages that deal with creation, or the end time, or heaven. The safest approach is to look for the basic message, avoiding a strict literal interpretation when the literary form is clearly symbolic, parabolic, or allegorical. The creation account of Genesis (1—3) is best viewed as God's revelation presenting answers to basic questions about human existence: Who created the world and everything in it? Who made man? What is the nature of man? Where did evil come from? The same might be said for Genesis 4—11, regarding questions such as: Does God judge wickedness? Is he merciful? How did God go about choosing Israel, the nation through whom he would reveal himself to mankind?

Similarly, passages dealing with the resurrection of the dead and the life to come are often expressed in highly symbolic language. Such passages in the gospels and epistles are difficult to harmonize in every detail. There is no reason why they should be. They present the material from several perspectives. The essential message is that life *does* continue beyond the grave. God *will* ultimately triumph in Christ at his appearing. This is the blessed hope that we look forward to with great anticipation.

Furthermore, when interpreting Scripture never base a doctrine on a single verse or a passage that is frought with difficulties. If the verse or passage isn't clear, it's best not to make too much of it. For example, the Mormon practice of baptizing the living for the dead has virtually no support in Scripture. It is based on one obscure, puzzling verse in 1 Corinthians (15:29).

Another example is the Jehovah's Witnesses' prohibition against blood transfusions, which is based on a bizarre interpretation of verses forbidding the eating of blood (Genesis 9:4; Leviticus 17:10-13; Acts 15:20).

When the Scriptures are silent on a specific practice, it is best to decide whether one should or should not adopt it on the basis of biblical principles. If a practice is not contrary to Scripture, if it will be beneficial to the individual concerned, to the church, and to society, then the practice is acceptable.

Fourth, when reading the Bible take time to find out who is writing and what the circumstances of the times were like. What was the author's purpose in writing? What were the historical circumstances in which he lived and wrote? Who is his audience? When interpreting a passage, note what precedes it, as well as what follows. When you're reading the epistles, notice whether it is a letter to an individual (such as Timothy, the young pastor/preacher) or to a church (such as the letter to the Hebrew Christians, or the church at Corinth). Avoid laying responsibility where it does not belong. For example, when Paul gives advice to Timothy about the proper qualifications for good church officers, or about what he should teach and preach, he is not necessarily speaking to members of the church, unless by implication. Notice, too, that most of our Lord's teachings and those of the apostles do not dwell on witnessing in the narrow evangelistic sense of that word. They address, instead, the basic nitty-gritty problems that confront us as Christians in everyday life within the church and the community. How should we live? How should we relate to one another?

I am not saying that we shouldn't witness by sharing the gospel on a personal level. I do this, and I know that you do, too. But what I am saying is that we should not magnify one aspect of the church's or Christian's responsibility out of all proportion. This is only a part of the individual Christian's and church's witness. If you would say that witnessing is *only* evangelism, I'd have to say that you're off base. Likewise, if you said that witnessing is *only* "doing good deeds," I'd have to say that you're off base again. The records in the Gospels demonstrate how our Lord beautifully combined conversation about God with "doing good," and likewise the book of Acts and the epistles show that the early church viewed both as essential.

I'm not really "doing good" when I give things for the body but withhold the life-giving message that would quicken the soul—restore it through new life in Christ. Neither am I "doing good" when I merely witness in word but refuse to give clothing and food to the individual who is cold and hungry (James 2:14-17; 1 John 3:16-18). As Christians we're obligated to live our whole life for Christ by ministering to others by word and deed.

Some Christians make others feel unnecessarily guilty for not being soul winners. They fail to observe that not everyone has the same spiritual gifts or abilities. In the church, the body of Christ, all gifts are regarded as essential to the proper functioning of the church. As Paul said in 1 Corinthians 12, "If the whole body were an eye, where would the sense of hearing be?" Or as I might say, "Tim, if everyone were an evangelist, who would do all the other tasks needed to sustain the total life of the church?"

Fifth, a word should be said about individual versus group insight into the meaning of the Scriptures. When God speaks to us through Scripture, prayer, meditation, or thought, he calls for a response of either "Yes, Lord," or "No, Lord." Either we will or we will not obey his command. But when you or I interpret Scripture, we dare not stand alone, defying the consensus of biblical scholarship handed down within the church through the centuries. Scripture, like the Holy Spirit, was given to the church, the body of believers. So if I say to you, "Tim, I interpret the passage this way, but *no one else* agrees with me," you can be fairly certain that I'm wrong. Quite often a majority have been wrong, but God has always preserved a "righteous remnant." This principle applies to biblical interpretation as well.

There is a great deal more that I could say about the Bible, but the important thing to keep in mind is that it is *the* written source of our knowledge of God. While Christians readily acknowledge that God's revelation of himself and his truth cannot be limited to the Bible, we believe that it is his special revelation to mankind. His will and purposes for us are to be found in it. It is "the only infallible rule of faith and practice" (behavior). The Bible is God's normative guide. We measure all else by it. In the Scriptures we find the progressive revelation of God, a revelation that reaches its zenith, apex, and fullness in the life and teachings of our Lord Jesus Christ (John 14:6-9; Colossians 1:15-20). He is the one by whom, or against which, all other teachings and belief systems must be judged. Whenever a teaching or principle conflicts with that of Christ, as Christians we stand with Jesus. Tim, I think you'll find, as I have found, that any ethical principle worth its salt will neither contradict the teachings of Christ nor those of Holy Scripture.

In summary, Tim, remember that interpreting the Bible properly should be prefaced by prayer for divine guidance. If you ask the Holy Spirit to enlighten you as you read the Word and as you draw upon the wealth of scholarly aids (Bible commentaries, dictionaries, histories, geographies, and lexicons of the original languages), he will help you. As you interpret passages, note the context—the passages before the one you're reading as well as those that follow—and read good commentaries to get the historical and cultural perspective. Take note also of the literary form being used, whether it's prose, poetry, parable, allegory, metaphor, simile, hyperbole, or apocalyptic literature. Be careful not to develop major doctrines on scanty evidence or on obscure passages. Concentrate on the bulk of Scripture that is relatively easy to understand, and don't waste time trying to "unscrew the inscrutable." And, Tim, compare your interpretation with that of the mainstream of Christian scholarship within the church.

Until later, then, the Lord be with you.

I love you, Tim,
Dad

Created in God's Image

Dear Tim,

While I teach sociology, I am convinced that religion, namely Christianity, is the most profitable discipline because it deals with ultimate questions. Furthermore, for the believer, Christianity is an interpretive and integrative thing—Christ and his teachings become our frame of reference, the one from which we take our cues for behavior. Sociology assumes that each human is born with a "clean slate." It assumes that human character and personality are formed by human interaction—a product of one's social environment (home, church, school, peer group)—and that cultural traits are all relative to specific cultures. I don't have any trouble with that, but it is only part of the truth.

Was mankind not created in the image of God? Wasn't human nature affected by "the fall?" Why is man, generically speaking, so evil? Has he always been this way? Can man experience a healthy wholeness in this life, or must his experience be one of continual frustration and despair? These are undoubtedly questions you've wondered about. They are questions that Christianity answers most satisfactorily.

When I was 18 years old, my parents lived in South Philadelphia. Late one night I was walking, looking at the shining stars and the full silvery moon. As I walked, I wondered, "What's it all about?" How small, how insignificant my life seemed in the face of the vastness of the heavens above. Where did I come from? Where was I going? About a year later your Aunt Rita introduced me to a friend of hers who helped me to make a commitment of my life to Christ. Then I began to understand what it was all about and began to find satisfying answers and meaning to life.

Who are we? Where did we come from? And where are we going? These are all crucial questions. Most people consciously or unconsciously are preoccupied with questions like that. Back in 1962 I participated in a youth conference at Oak Ridge, Tennessee. We spent the weekend hearing various lectures about the space program and the possibility of life on other planets. On the way home the young people in my car raised questions not about "outer space," but "inner space." They wanted to know about themselves, about God, and Christ. They wanted to find the meaning of life.

But I'm afraid some persons are unwilling to face the hard questions, or they just don't know how or where to begin to find answers.

When we think about the origin and place of humans in the world, Christianity usually answers questions such as "who," "why," and "how," in one of two ways. Generally there is little disagreement among Christians on "who" and "why." They believe that God created humans in his image. Likewise, they agree that we were created for fellowship with God and one another. Where Christians differ, however, is at the point of "how" God did it.

Most conservative Christians believe that God created

man as man—a separate, unique species.

However, many other Christians believe that humankind emerged from a diverging species of the *primate* order. They associate the concept of man being created in the image of God with that point in time when this particular species became "human"—when it developed the physical, mental, and spiritual attributes we associate with personhood. More specifically, they think of the point at which the creature began to reflect on his own nature and his relationship to God.

On the other hand, some non-Christians do not associate God with "who," "why," or "how." They reject the entire notion that God created the human race. It seems to me that the atheistic position takes more faith—believing that we just evolved or appeared by chance, without any activity on God's part. This is like believing a jumbo jet just evolved and took to the air without the aid of aeronautical engineers and skilled craftsmen. Believing we are children of God, created in his image, requires a faith commitment. But not to believe requires not only an act of faith, but also a denial of that which seems logical and rational.

You and I have never talked about evolution, probably because it never was a problem for either of us. I frankly don't feel threatened by the various theories that have been proposed. They are attempts to answer *how*, that is, the process by which the world and man got here. Scientists cannot answer *why*—only religion can really answer that. While no one can speak with certainty about *how* man became man, I find that the insights of science enhance faith rather than diminish it. A theory of *how* need not be in conflict with the Christian belief in God as Creator.

Tim, you'll find that most Christians probably have not read or thought much about the matter. Even though they do not believe that man evolved from some protohuman, they do recognize the fact that change takes place all the time. God created mankind and the world and he continues to direct and sustain them. But, as I mentioned above, conservative Christians often draw the line at the notion of the evolution of man. They insist that the Genesis account of creation clearly states that man was a unique creation of God. He has always existed as man. He is the highest of God's creation. This is not to say that lower forms of animal life are not important, but that there is a rank order to creation—God, man, and animals. Man alone was created in the "image of God." He alone enjoys the unique privilege of fellowship with God.

I can empathize with them, Tim, but those who reject the evolutionary concept should realize that the *theistic* evolutionist in no way denies man's uniqueness. Nor does he deny the concept of "the fall." Fortunately, our salvation doesn't depend on which interpretation of *how* we select. It's good to remember this, not only in relation to this question, but also in relation to other issues on which Christians hold differing opinions. Let me move on.

Undoubtedly you're asking, "Dad, just what do you mean when you say that man was created in the image of God? What sort of ideas do you include?" Tim, before I suggest some things that I think are implicit in that concept, let me say that when we think about God, we can only speak anthropomorphically. That is, we can only use human terms and analogies—we can only infer from our experience and from what is revealed about God in Scripture. However, the crucial difference between God and man is this: in a limited or finite way we possess some of the attributes of God, but he possesses them and others in a perfect and infinite manner (Psalm 18:30).

44

Certainly one of the attributes we associate with the concept of the "image of God" is rationality. We are rational, reflective beings. Just as God is a rational being capable of reflective thought, one who is not subject to fluctuations of uncontrollable emotions, so we are capable of rational thought and behavior. I think that you demonstrate this rather well, Tim. You're a thoughtful person. You don't go off "half-cocked," like Don Quixote, riding off in all directions—acting first and thinking later. The more rational we are, the more we resemble our Creator.

Second, man is also a reflective being. He can "stand off and look at himself." I'm sure you've done this. Sometimes in the quietness of your inner self you've made a critical appraisal of "where you've come from, and where you're going." Maybe you've even caught a reflective moment in an apparent time of crisis—when you encountered a problem riding your trail bike or while skiing. Or maybe it happened just as you were awaking before your car hit that tree! More than likely, though, you've had meaningful moments of reflection while alone, when you've reviewed aspects of your past as you contemplated future decisions.

Third, man has a free will. He doesn't *have to* do anything, just as God is not compelled to do anything. God is free to do as he pleases. But being a righteous, just, holy, and rational being, he always acts in a manner consistent with his own nature. Unfortunately, man is not as consistent. Nonetheless, he is still free to choose.

Now there is a sense in which it appears as if the events and the course of our lives are determined. The decisions we make do have future consequences. As we think and act in certain ways, we seem to commit ourselves to think and behave increasingly in a given direction. For example, by concentrating on skiing you have given more and more time to training, to competitions, and to teaching your friends how to ski. Therefore, when you're confronted with options about reading, socializing, and working, it seems "natural" to make decisions that facilitate your career in skiing. Choices do have consequences. So think through your options carefully, considering both the intended and unintended consequences of your decisions.

But despite the fact that our thoughts and behavior become channeled in a certain direction, anywhere along the line we are free to redirect them. We can change our mind. Anthony convicted as a pickpocket, was converted while in prison. His life was completely changed—he did an about face. While it is more difficult to break patterns of behavior that are long established (my tendency to get loud when I get excited), it can be done. We are free *and* we are responsible.

Tim, this point is quite important. No doubt you've come across people who blame society, the establishment, or God for the adversity in their lives. No one in his right mind would deny that our society has inequities. *All* societies— even countries that build walls to keep people in "because it's good for them"—are inequitable. Society is composed of sinful, selfish·individuals. Some recognize their condition and try to overcome it; others do not. Actually, I'm amazed that our society is as just and equitable as it is. In part, I believe this is because our society adheres to basic Judeo-Christian principles, and in part it is because of the large proportion of committed Christians. But it's not society, the establishment, or God who is primarily responsible for a person's condition—it is the individual. My mother used to say to us children, "*You* make your bed, and *you* have to lie in it." She never allowed us to excuse our failures and mistakes by projecting the blame onto others.

As a sociologist I'm well aware of the influence and social control exercised by groups, organizations, institutions, and the state on our life. But in the final analysis, aside from congenital defects and accidents beyond our control, we are the ones who make the choices that determine our destiny. It seems to me, Tim, that if we are not free to choose, then there is no way we can be held accountable for our actions.

I almost forgot another important point about freedom. Often people ask, "Why didn't God create us so we *could not* sin?" Perhaps you've raised the same question, thinking that this would have eliminated sickness, disease, and suffering. The answer to that serious question is a traditional one, but the best one I know. If man is to be free, and not a mere puppet on a string, then he must have freedom to disobey God, as well as obey him. He must have the freedom to live cooperatively and responsibly in community, or uncooperatively and irresponsibly. Virtue is virtue only when it is freely offered. Those who criticize God for granting us "freedom of choice" are the same ones who harp on the need for individual freedom. In the overall scheme of things we have to accept the bitter with the sweet.

Fourth, human beings have the capacity to create—not on the same scale as God, obviously. But, nonetheless, we were commanded by God to "subdue" and "have dominion" over all the earth. (As Christian environmentalists rightly point out, this is not a license to abuse, exploit, and waste.) The creativity of mankind has been a mixed blessing. On the one hand, so much has been created to improve the quality of life; but on the other hand, so much has been done that is destructive. The nuclear and electronic revolutions can either make earth a heaven or a hell. Given man's inherent tendency to be self-centered and exploitive in his relationships with others, we have real cause for alarm and good reason to keep a close watch on things. But my point here is that God made us with a brain that can, if used properly, bring to fruition all kinds of blessings in every field of endeavor.

Fifth, man is a spiritual being. This is the difference between man and the animals in the Genesis account. "God formed man from the dust of the ground and breathed into his nostrils the breath of life, and man became a living being" (Genesis 2:7). Most biblical scholars believe that man *in totality* is a living soul. We differentiate between flesh and spirit for purposes of discussion, just as we often talk about mind and body. But man is not three separate entities—body, soul, and spirit. He is a body/spirit—a living soul. God and humans can communicate because we were created in his image or likeness.

We are not "a part of God" as the pantheist would say. They believe that the grass, the trees, the stars are all *part of* God. We don't believe that when a person or a tree dies, God is diminished. God is an *infinite*, spiritual, personal being who is separate from his creation. He doesn't have a "body," as the Mormons contend. He's not the "big man in the sky." We are *finite*, spiritual beings, clothed in a flesh that is *good*, although the flesh has been weakened by "the fall" (we'll get to that concept later). It is because we have this spiritual nature, this affinity with God, that God and man can communicate with each other (1 Corinthians 2:9-16; Acts 17:27-28).

Sixth, being created in the image of God means that the attributes that are inherent in God's personality in an infinite, perfect way, can be developed in us on a finite scale. I was going to say that we are emotional beings, but that is not exactly what I had in mind. I'm thinking of qualities such as love, mercy, forgiveness, justice, holiness, and I guess we

48

should include hate and wrath. If we are created in his image, certainly this includes a capacity to express our emotions in these ways. But whereas I, as you too well know, lose my temper at times and do and say things I'm sorry for later, *God never loses control.* Since he's perfect in knowledge, wisdom, and understanding, and since he is beyond time, God is never surprised or taken aback by anything that happens.

But, nonetheless, he does "feel"—he has what I would call perfect "empathic ability." He can put himself in our shoes and understand our plight. The incarnation of God in Christ is testimony to this fact. God is touched with the feelings of our infirmities (Isaiah 49:15; Lamentations 3:22-32; Micah 7:19; Hebrews 4:15; 5:2). He remembers our frame—our makeup. He knows that we are "dust" (Psalm 103:14). So just as God empathizes with us, just as he loves the good and hates evil, just as he's merciful and compassionate, and just as he is forgiving and reconciling, so we have these capacities within us. And we should work to develop them in a mature, responsible manner.

Tim, I didn't realize I'd get so involved here. But let me tie these thoughts together. Man was created in the image of God. God infused man's flesh with a spirit, and man became a living soul or being. The finite attributes we bear are similar to those we associate with the personality of the infinite God. While God embodies them fully and perfectly, we embody them partially and imperfectly. We are like God in that we are rational and reflective beings. We have freedom of choice—either to obey or disobey God. While our character and personality are influenced and formed through interaction with others, ultimately we are responsible for our behavior and development. Futhermore, God has endowed us with the ability to create. We are spiritual beings and, therefore, we can fellowship and commune with God. And as God expresses the attributes of love, mercy, forgiveness, justice, holiness, and wrath, so may we. Finally, Tim, just as God empathizes and ministers to us, we are expected to do the same for one another (Galatians 6:2; John 13:12-15; 34-35; Romans 12:14-21).

I'll sign off for now. I'll pick up with some more thoughts about the nature of man in my next letter.

I pray for you daily, Tim. Take care.

All my love,
Dad

Human Nature and the Fall

Dear Tim,

In my last letter I said that man is unique, created in God's image. In this letter I'd like to share some thoughts on "human nature." I have already referred to the fact that men and women are not just another type of animal, but are the highest order of God's creation. We are basically spiritual beings, created for fellowship with God and one another. As Saint Augustine said, "Thou has formed us for thyself, and our hearts are restless till they rest in thee."

This point was driven home as I read of the death of Barbara Hutton, heiress to the F. W. Woolworth fortune. A millionaire, she lived a lonely, unhappy life. She confessed, "You can't buy love with money." She married seven times, but could not find the happiness she desperately sought. Tragically, Hutton and many others, rich and poor, have learned too late that a man's life does not consist in the abundance of his possessions" (Luke 12:15). We *cannot* satisfy the hunger of the soul with *things*.

Many people don't think you can talk about "human nature" as an entity, consisting of basic attributes and needs. But others, myself included, think that you can. It seems to me that all persons have basic needs, and these must be met if we are to function in a healthy way. Of course the fall marred the image of God in us, and consequently human nature was affected, too. I'll discuss the concept of the fall later in this chapter.

Tim, before suggesting some basic qualities that I believe are characteristic of all humans, whether aborigines or aristocrats, let me say a few things about the conscience. Man is the only one of God's creatures that has a conscience. When we are born, we *assume* that no specific notions of "right" or "wrong" are constituent parts of our conscience. Nonetheless, I believe that inherent in the "raw stuff" of conscience is a sense of morality—right and wrong that is God-given (Romans 2:15; Galatians 5:16-25; Romans 7:21-25; 5:12, 18-19). It is generally agreed, however, that through the process of socialization the conscience develops—by parents, siblings, and others responding to the child and the child responding to them. Therefore, what constitutes acceptable behavior will vary from culture to culture, since each is unique.

But regardless of the society into which we're born each of us will develop a sense of what is "right" and "wrong." The laws about morality and human behavior will vary, depending on the knowledge base, and the religious and political philosophies that inform and undergird that society. The fact that all societies, regardless of their ideologies, have notions of right and wrong, suggests to me that God is "out there" impinging upon us. It's not just the fact that all peoples have some standard of right and wrong, but within societies where immoral ways are accepted as "normal," there are always those who march to the beat of a different drummer—those who speak out with prophetic conviction attempting to turn things around. So God has not abandoned man. Even though the conscience has been marred by the fall and is not completely trustworthy, God speaks to us through his Spirit, seeking to reconcile us to himself (John 16:7-11).

Now let me suggest several basic needs all human beings have that are necessary for the development of a relatively well-balanced personality. (I'm indebted to W. I. Thomas, a sociologist, who expressed these ideas decades ago.)

First of all, we need to feel loved and wanted. We need to feel secure—like we belong. Ultimately our capacity to love comes from God, but this is mediated to us through our experience within the family (1 John 4:19). This love is conveyed not only verbally and with hugs and kisses, but also by consistent discipline. Just as God loves and disciplines his children, so does the good parent (Hebrews 12:5-6).

When I was in elementary school there was a period when I felt unloved at home. This was probably because your Uncle Tom and Uncle Tony came along to take all of grandmom's attention! With six kids between sixteen and two years of age to wrestle with, living in a small row house, and trying to feed and clothe us all on a limited income, it's a wonder she did as well as she did. Anyway, I must have complained to my third-grade schoolteacher, Mrs. Gross. She said, "You can come and live with me." When I went home that day, grandmom was down in the basement washing clothes in a galvanized tub on one of those old-fashioned corrugated washboards. I said, "Mom, Mrs. Gross said that I can go home and live with her." I don't remember what she said, but I can still feel the thrashing I got. While it hurt, there was no doubt in my mind that she did love me—and I had a red bottom to prove it!

Your mom and I haven't been perfect parents by a long

shot, but I hope we've conveyed our love for you kids and that you feel secure in it. When I think of some of the frank discussions we've had—some heated, others calm—I guess you must have felt secure or you wouldn't have spoken so frankly and forcefully. You've probably forgotten, but I remember the time when you were taking "Problems in Democracy" and you were studying stocks and bonds. You told me in no uncertain terms that I was a failure. If I had had any sense I would have invested my money—played the stock market. Boy, if I had spoken to my father like that, I'd be picking myself up off the floor! But you were a near-adult then, and you were entitled to your opinion.

Another important thing that we all need is recognition. We're all unique individuals. No two of us are alike. You're different from Steve, Steve's different from Debbi, and Debbi's different from Susan. We didn't treat you all alike, because you're not alike. Sometimes you may have felt like complaining, "Dad and mom like Steve more than me." But because we treated each of you as a unique individual, that's the risk we took. We tried to recognize each of your strengths, and correct, overlook, or accept your weaknesses just as I hope you'll accept ours. All people need this recognition and acceptance. But, unfortunately, many children are unloved and rejected by their parents; many do not receive the recognition and support they need to develop in a healthy fashion.

In addition to personal recognition, everyone is entitled to a positive response. We need the affirmation of others. We need to know that those who love us think that we're "okay." This includes mutual trust and respect that helps us accomplish the goals and projects that are important to us. The worst thing one can experience is indifference and apathy. In many ways it's worse than hate and hostility. At least someone who is hostile toward you is acknowledging that you exist. But no response at all is hard to accept. Again, mom and I have tried to give you the support you need. There were times when we weren't convinced of the wisdom of some of your ventures—such as buying that trail bike. And should I mention kayaking alone? Forget it!

In addition to a positive response, Tim, we all need a creative outlet. Whether it's a job, skill, profession, or a creative hobby such as sports, arts, or music, we all need to feel that we're making a contribution to others. Unless one feels that he is doing something worthwhile, his self-image and self-confidence won't amount to much. I suspect that's why being unemployed has such a devastating effect upon people. Furthermore, this may explain why people move from one job or career to another. They are trying to gain status and recognition. Everyone wants to be "somebody."

Still another basic need is for new experiences to keep spice in our lives. Fellowship with Christ and service in the church offers an excellent creative outlet. If you don't take advantage of opportunities for creative new experiences, you'll go stale and become bored. Your religious experience will level off and deteriorate. This happened to me in the 1960s. I became somewhat inactive and I found myself getting unduly critical. Fortunately a friend said, "Well, Charlie, what on earth are you doing?" I needed that prod! I needed to get actively involved. I needed new experiences of fellowship and service. The non-Christian lacks that spiritual dimension which I think is so essential. Even though his life may be "one new experience after another," apart from Christ it's difficult to find real inner spiritual satisfaction (Jeremiah 2:13; John 7:38-39; Philippians 3:8-12).

All of us have basic needs. If these needs aren't met, a person will not develop properly. He will seek unhealthy modes of expression to compensate for the lack of love, trust, recognition, or sense of belonging in his life. He may become suspicious and distrustful. He may become aggressive and strike out at others. Or he may turn his hostility on himself or withdraw into his shell. The point is, that we are socialized into being human. Most of us by virtue of birth into a caring family develop into outgoing, positive people; others, due to no fault of their own, are maladjusted.

However, whether we develop a healthy conscience with a proper sense of "right and wrong," or whether we develop less ideally, we are all finite creatures who are tainted with Adam's fallen nature (Romans 5:12-19).

I have emphasized our basic human needs. Now I want to suggest some reasons why individuals do not develop wholesomely, with well-adjusted personalities.

The Bible teaches that in Adam each of us has experienced the fall, and that as a result human nature has been marred. I'm sure you've heard people say, "It's *only human nature* to take all you can get." "Man is *by nature* polygamous." "It's *only natural* to seek revenge." You'll never find secular sociologists or psychologists talking about the fall because theoretically it is a religious belief. But it can be demonstrated that all *act* as if there were a fall. It is an empirical fact that *all* people are by nature sinful and self-centered (Isaiah 53:6a; Jeremiah 17:9; Romans 3:23). The Christian believes that this empirically verifiable fact stems from the fall (Romans 5:12).

Man's alienated condition—alienation from himself, others, and God—stems from Adam's rebellion against God. The name Adam means *man*, and he symbolizes every man. The account of Adam and Eve's rebellion in the Garden of Eden explains how our sinful natures originated. If one rejects this explanation, he nonetheless demonstrates by his

56

behavior that he is a member of a "fallen" race.

By rebelling, man sought to be free from God, to become equal with God and usurp his place. This, however, did not result in freedom, but in the fall and alienation. God made us for harmonious interaction with himself and one another, but man's pride and inordinate self-love, or self-centeredness, disrupted the intended harmony. As a result we face all sorts of personal and societal problems (James 4:1-2).

The serpent in the Genesis account symbolizes the devil. Interestingly, Tim, the serpent only has power to suggest, not power to coerce. Just as the devil appeared as a serpent, he takes many forms and shapes. At different times and stages in the human life cycle evil confronts us through individuals and desires (he-she-or-it), seeking to lead us away from God. The apostle James makes clear, however, that it is *not* God who tempts us. Instead, we allow ourselves to be tempted, seduced, "lured and enticed by our own desires" (James 1:13-15). So in a sense, we are our own worst enemy. I'm back to that notion of personal responsibility again. So while we are descendants of Adam, and the devil does tempt us, we are responsible for our own sinning (Romans 5:12; 1 Peter 5:8; James 1:13-15).

Tim, when I talk of human sin, I don't necessarily mean physical misbehavior of the grossest kind. Perhaps the biggest sin is *pride* and it was exemplified by Adam and Eve. I don't mean the legitimate sense of pride you take in a job well done, but exaggerated, falsely based pride (Romans 12:3; 1 Corinthians 4:7). The biggest sin isn't a sexual one (pre- or extra-marital sex); it isn't drunkenness, drug abuse, or theft. I don't minimize them for a minute. They seriously disrupt the lives of individuals, families, and friends, as well as the community. But, as I mentioned in my first letter, the biggest sin is arrogantly dismissing God with a wave of the hand saying, "I don't need him!" Or worse, it is refusing to acknowledge that he exists. Unbelief and ingratitude are identified as twin sins that lead to idolatry and immorality (Romans 1:20-22). Some of the worst sinners are not on skid row or in the ghetto. They are nice, clean-cut, impeccably dressed, respectable, intellectual folks on college and university campuses, in business and government offices. They are persons who refuse humbly to recognize God as their Creator, Judge, and Redeemer. Despite their arrogance and ingratitude, Paul says they will someday fall on their knees and acknowledge that Jesus Christ is Lord (Philippians 2:10-11).

You know the old trick. People begin to talk about the hypocrites in the church, about the sins of professing Christians—as if Christians ever made any claim to perfection. I suppose their criticism is designed to extract from us an attitude of awe and reverence in the presence of their impeccable moral example. In reality, it's a cowardly way of not facing up to their own sins and shortcomings. It's the old "Pharisee and the publican" routine all over again (Luke 18:9-14). Any fool can find someone worse than himself. But if Christ is accepted as the standard of righteousness, it's impossible to come away "smelling like a rose." Pride, rebellion, and ingratitude were the insidious sins that caused Adam and Eve to fall, and they are still causing individuals to fall today.

Tim, another point I should make is that the effect of the fall was pervasive (Genesis 6:5; Jeremiah 17:9; Titus 1:15; Romans 3:10-18). Sometimes Christians use the expression *total depravity*. That sounds awful doesn't it? And it is. This simply means that *all* areas and aspects of life have been affected. Kenneth Foreman, my theology professor at Louisville Presbyterian Seminary, said that just as a drop of ink in a glass of water permeates every molecule, so the fall affects all aspects of our lives.

This doesn't mean that man is *all* "bad." Man was created in the image of God, and God was pleased with what he created (Genesis 1:31). Man is really a mixture of good and evil. The apostle Paul, reflecting the Jewish teachings of his day, talked about the inner struggle between the *flesh* and the *spirit* that goes on in each of us (Galatians 5:16-17; Romans 7:7-25; 8:1-11). While the fall and our subsequent personal rebellion resulted in our alienation and estrangement from God, we can still communicate with him. It is because of this contact with God that we are aware that something is wrong inside of ourselves, as well as outside. Furthermore, how could we respond to the appeal of the gospel if the fall resulted in our complete alienation and separation from God?

Some Christians are unwilling to admit that fallen man has any good in him. But that seems ridiculous to me. We are still God's children, even if estranged.

It's interesting, Tim, how the fall affects our perception of reality, especially as we try to isolate and identify the causes of the corruption and exploitation in the world today. The Marxist faults the capitalist system controlled by the rich and the powerful who exploit and oppress the worker. He also faults the church for diverting man's attention to the next world and for remaining silent in the face of such oppression and exploitation. The Marxist answer is to get rid of capitalism and Christianity and replace them with the "dictatorship of the proletariat" (the workers) and atheism. (As if all "workers" are saints and all businessmen are sinners, and as if all within the church are scoundrels and all atheists live by the Golden Rule!) We have seen enough of the results of communist regimes to know that "the devil" wasn't destroyed by replacing business elites, imperfect democracy, and the church with political elites, totalitarianism, and soulless religious surrogates.

Furthermore, the Christian church is not a monolithic structure. While some segments of it have abandoned their prophetic role, many have not. Instead of being an opiate or drug, making people content with their lot, it has really been the catalyst which has modified capitalism and produced a more equitable democratic society. Today you could argue that the real opiate is Marxist materialism that attempts to delude the masses by offering them a mess of pottage in an attempt to get them to ignore their inner spiritual hunger and need. I must add, however, that much of our capitalist consumer society attempts to do the same thing!

The point that I want to make is that playing political or economic musical chairs is not the answer to our basic needs. The answer lies in acknowledging that each individual has been affected by the fall, and that nothing short of personal renewal through reconciliation to God in Christ will effect significant changes in corporate society. *Neither* capitalism *nor* socialism, per se, is the culprit. It's sin operating in fallen man.

Well, Tim, I'll stop at this point. Summing up, then, humans alone have a conscience that serves as a point of contact between God and man. From conception the rudiments of conscience are there, but conscience is further developed through interaction with family members and others. Human nature requires that we be loved and wanted, receive recognition and be responded to, and that we have a creative outlet, as well as an opportunity for new experiences. But even if an individual is reared in a wholesome, supportive family, he still reflects the results of the fall. We are estranged and alienated from God—the image of God in us has been marred. The effect of the fall is pervasive, so that all aspects of our lives are tainted with excessive self-interest—*sin*. Pride, ingratitude, and unbelief—the spiritual sins—are the most destructive kind. Man's problem is not primarily external—political, economic, or social. The problem is internal—within man himself. But thank God, by accepting God's offer of forgiveness in Christ we can have the image of God restored in us. We can become new creations in Christ Jesus (2 Corinthians 5:17).

Goodby for now, Tim. In my next letter I'll share some thoughts about the nature of God. God bless and keep you.

All my love,
Dad

Foundational Assumptions About God

Dear Tim,

In my last two letters, I shared with you some basic concepts about mankind—the image of God, human nature, and the fall. In the next couple of letters I want to share some thoughts about the nature of God.

In talking about God, Tim, we can approach the topic from either a philosophical or a religious perspective. The fundamental difference is that religion is based on revelation. We make two basic assumptions as Christians: first, *God is;* and second, *he has revealed himself.* As I mentioned in an earlier letter, the Bible contains the historical unfolding of God's nature, will, and purpose for mankind. His full and final revelation is focused in Jesus Christ. Philosophy, theoretically at least, begins its search from scratch, rejecting revelation. Christians, however, accept this revelation of God in Scripture and engage in both inductive and deductive study of it to learn what he has to say.

Our faith in God, however, is not only based on the revelation of God in Scripture. You and I (and countless others) have personally experienced him. Thomas Jefferson said that "revelation that is secondhand is only hearsay."

When you all were kids we read you Bible stories. You believed them. But when you grew older, each of you experienced God for yourselves as you gave your heart to Christ. This changed your whole attitude toward the Bible. Now it is no longer a secondhand revelation about God. Now you read the Bible from a new perspective. You can identify with the experiences of God's people in Scripture in a new way. Their experience of sin, rebellion, repentance, confession, forgiveness, reconciliation, joy, new life, and suffering become yours. The Bible, while historically the Word of God to man, has taken on a new dimension. It has become God's *personal* revelation to you. As you read the Bible ask, "Lord, how does this apply to me today?" He will speak to you through its pages. Once we have received God's redemption and committed our lives to Christ, we can understand the enthusiasm of Blaise Pascal, noted French philosopher and mathematician. After he experienced God in Christ, he wrote:

> The year of grace, 1654
> Monday, 25 November . . .
> From about half past ten in the evening until about half past twelve,
> .FIRE. . . . .
> God of Abraham, God of Isaac, God of Jacob, not of the philosophers and scholars.
> Certitude, certitude, feeling, joy, peace.
> *God of Jesus Christ.*
> My God and your God.

I was talking to Robin Protheroe, lecturer in religion at Trent Polytechnic, about Sigmund Freud's criticism that Christians *project* God "out there" because we want the security of a "cosmic father." (Of course you can turn that right around and say, "You *reject* God 'out there' because you want to ignore his demands on your life.") The Christian's response is that *God is.* He created us; we didn't create him. He revealed himself to us. Furthermore, Freud was merely pointing out a normal human mental process. Projection and analogous thinking are God-given modes of thinking and communicating. They are normal thought processes. Furthermore, we use the language of simile and metaphor to convey our beliefs, feelings, and spiritual experiences all the time. We don't create reality through thought, but we use various mental processes to describe and communicate reality and interpret its meaning. I hope this is helpful.

One of the basic truths is that God is a *person,* albeit an infinite person (Exodus 3:14; Psalm 45:3; Jeremiah 23:23-24). He is not an impersonal, nondescript "force." God is an infinite being, a spiritual being who embodies all the attributes we associate with the ideal person, only he possesses them in a perfect state (John 4:24). I say *him,* but the Bible uses many analogies to describe God. In reality God is an androgynous being—neither male nor female. "He" embodies all the qualities we identify with the ideal father and mother. While father is the predominant descriptive adjective used in the Bible, we do find mother, king, rock, holy one, and others used to describe God. Of course our Lord Jesus reveals the personal nature of God and he embodies all that God wished to reveal to us—even though humanly speaking he was a male (John 1:18; 14:6-11).

In the New Testament several words—predicate nouns—are used to characterize God. The apostle John said, "God is *light*" (1 John 1:5). Embodied in the concept of light is the revelation of *truth.* Equating God and light suggests that he is all knowing, omniscient. The association between light and revelation can be seen in the experience of Moses at the burning bush (Exodus 3:1-14). God shows himself as one who spends himself for his people and yet is never spent. Furthermore, God the light, chose to reveal himself to us in Jesus, the light of the world, who "enlightens every man" who comes into the world (John 8:12: 1:5). We, in turn, are expected to become the light of God in the world (Matthew 5:14; Ephesians 5:8; 1 Thessalonians 5:5; 1 John 2:10).

God is omniscient (Romans 11:33-34; Psalm 147:5). He knows the beginning and the end. He is the Alpha and the Omega (Revelation 1:8). Since God knows all, some think that this means everything is fixed, that our behavior has been predetermined, that we have been programmed. But God is not a product of time. Time was created by him. In our world everything is inevitably thought of in terms of a cause-effect relationship. We are creatures of time. But God sees everything as an eternal now. Yet, since we were created with freedom to choose, our life will unfold as we choose either to cooperate with his revealed will, or reject it and go our own way (James 1:14; 4:7; Deuteronomy 30:19; Romans 7:12-13; 12:1-2).

Not only is God light, but Jesus said that God is Spirit (John 4:24). This helps some by eliminating false ideas about God. He is not, as the Mormons suggest, clothed with a physical body. This would not only confine the Almighty but, worst of all, it would make him a finite creature. On the positive side, the concept of God as a personal *spiritual* being helps us understand his omnipresence. We can grasp in some measure how the one infinite God can be everywhere at the same time. But, having said that, I realize that it is difficult for us to understand fully the nature of God (Isaiah 55:8-9; Romans 11:33-36). We accept that he is an infinite, personal spirit and being by faith (Hebrews 11:6). He is one whom we have experienced, and all we can say to others is, "O taste and see that the Lord is good" (Psalm 34:8)!

Not only is God light and Spirit, but John says that God is *love* (1 John 4:8). We derive our capacity to love from him. He pours out his love on all—the good and the evil (Matthew 5:44-48). The agnostic and the atheist, as well as the one who curses God, are not beyond the reach of God's love. Our Lord Jesus revealed the magnitude of God's love when he hung on the cross and interceded to the Father on behalf of those who crucified him. He said, "Father, forgive them, for they do not know what they are doing" (Luke 23:24). This kind of love is superhuman, all-encompassing, mind-boggling! It is this kind of love God gives to those who are truly committed to Christ (Romans 5:5; 2 Timothy 1:7).

But God is *just,* as well as loving (Deuteronomy 32:4; 1 John 1:9). He doesn't play favorites. He is impartial in his judgment (Psalm 119:75a). Human justice seems to be partial and defers to the rich and powerful. We bend the law to suit ourselves, and human justice permits the favored to get away with murder. But God is no respecter of persons. He uses one standard to judge us all—the standard of righteousness revealed in Jesus Christ (Acts 10:34; Romans 2:16; 1 Peter 1:17).

God is also omnipresent—he is everywhere. Tennyson said, "Closer is he than breathing, nearer than hands and feet." The psalmist says there is no place we can go where we would lose his kindly presence and helpful power. It doesn't matter if we ascend the heights of heaven or descend to the place of the dead, God is there (Psalm 139:7-12). The experience of the prophet Jonah teaches us that. The awareness of God's omnipresence, as well as his omnipotence and onmiscience, ought not to be a dreadful thought, but a comforting and reassuring one (Psalm 139:1-6).

God isn't a party pooper or a killjoy. He's not out to spoil our fun. He stands as a just and loving Father who forgives the penitent and gives strength to the weak. Tim, this is so very important. It's a point we tried to emphasize within the family. When any of us wronged another, we always felt secure enough within our relationship to admit our wrong and forgive one another. We didn't hold grudges, did we? When we forgive and renew strained relationships, we are following God's example in Christ. We don't have to run and hide from an angry, wrathful God. He eagerly awaits the humble penitent to forgive and restore (Isaiah 55:6-8; Luke 15:20-24). Tremendous, isn't it! God is not only our Creator, and our Judge, but is also our Redeemer. I'll write about this later on.

Tim, one of the problem areas associated with belief in God is the problem of evil. How do you reconcile the notion that God is just and caring with the presence of so much evil in the world today? Boy, that's a tough one. I just talked to a colleague today whose three-year-old child has leukemia. How on earth do you convince him that God, the all-powerful God is also a loving God? How do you tell Christians, Jews, and others who suffered and whose relatives were killed in Russia, Germany, Uganda, Iran, Vietnam, Cambodia, South Africa, or wherever that God is love? How do you convince oppressed and deprived minorities in every nation that God loves them as much as he loves the controlling majority? Furthermore, how do you reconcile catastrophic earthquakes, volcano eruptions like Mount Saint Helens, hurricanes, and tornadoes with a loving Father?

Oddly enough, I talked to Alan Jones shortly after I met my friend whose child has leukemia. I asked him, "How do you reconcile this with the God of love?" He shared with me that his youngest son, Stephen, was sick and suffering severely when he was just ten months old. Alan said that he knelt by his son's bed and committed him to God's care. He said, "There was even a time when I prayed that God would take him. He was suffering so much I couldn't bear it. This is where our faith comes in," Alan continued. "God *is* a God of love and he knows best and we *must* trust." Indeed, Tim, this is the mystery which is beyond our understanding! In the end, it is, as Alan Jones said, a matter of trust.

But I wish I knew, Tim! While the apostle Paul said, "All things work together for good," he didn't say that all things that happen to us *are* good (Romans 8:28). Our Lord didn't venture to explain why some are born blind or why some experience tragedy in their lives (John 9:1ff.; Luke 13:1-5). Even he had to bear the cup of bitter suffering. While he prayed that he might be delivered, he concluded by saying, "Yet not what I will, but what you will" (Mark 14:32-36). But God does promise to be with us when we "walk through the valley of the shadow of death" (Psalm 23:4). Or, as Isaiah put it, "When you pass through the waters, I will be with you...When you walk through the fire, you will not be burned; the flames will not set you ablaze" (43:2). While some people *are* literally overwhelmed and consumed, God does give those who trust him a deep-seated inner peace and assurance (Isaiah 26:3; John 14:27; 16:33; Philippians 4:5-7).

What do we fall back on? How do we cope? We just hold on and trust, like Alan did—and like the family of Chester Bitterman did. You recall he was the Wycliffe Bible translator who was murdered in Colombia, South America.

Tim, before leaving this problem of God and illness, I should say a word about God and faith healing. From a Christian perspective all healing is *divine* healing. Through a variety of means God works to heal and restore to health those who are ill. Modern medicine is one of the crucial instruments God uses to facilitate healing. But in addition to the medical arts, the patient's faith, as well as the faith of family and friends, plays an important part in the healing process (Mark 2:5; Luke 17:11-19).

But having faith doesn't necessarily mean that one will be physically healed. Jesus never promised us that discipleship meant that we would not suffer illnesses and eventually die—as I mentioned earlier. Indeed, he said the opposite. The *cross*, not a "bed of roses," is the symbol of Christianity (Luke 9:23). The apostles and other early Christians were well aware of this, as are hundreds of thousands living in totalitarian states that deny religious freedom. The disciples followed Christ, not because he promised freedom from sickness, pain, and hardship, but because he offered them the gospel. He offered them forgiveness, fellowship with God and other believers, the dynamic of the Holy Spirit, and a chance to serve (Luke 24:45-49; Mark 8:34-38; Matthew 28:16-20). While healing the sick was an integral part of the ministry of Jesus, the apostles, and the early church, they didn't pervert and distort the gospel as some faith healers do today. Some of these are wolves in sheep's clothing, men and women out to make a fast buck (more likely a fast few hundred thousand) at the expense of desperate, helpless people (Matthew 7:15-20; 2 Corinthians 11:13-15). You can tell by their accumulated wealth that they bear little resemblance to our Lord who had nowhere to lay his head (Matthew 8:20).

Tim, suppose two people had cancer. Both were devout Christians. One died within three months of diagnosis. The other experienced a miraculous remission and lived for ten more years. Does this mean the one who died within three months had no faith? Is that why he died? Does this mean that God didn't love the one who died within three months? The modern, irresponsible *Elmer Gantry* (the phony faith healer) would try to have us believe that. The truth of the matter is that God loved them both. We just don't know why he receives some into his presence before others (Luke 13:1-5; 2 Corinthians 5:1, 8).

If you look at Scripture you'll find that some individuals were healed or delivered from death, while others were not healed, or they died a premature or martyr's death (Hebrews 11:8-38). While God prolonged the life of king Hezekiah by fifteen years, he allowed king Josiah to be struck down in battle at age thirty-nine (2 Kings 20:1-19; 2 Chronicles 35:23-24). While Job recovered from his plague of boils and had his prosperity restored to him, Jeremiah the prophet was severely persecuted and suffered continuously (Job 42:12-16; Jeremiah). God refused to heal the apostle Paul of his affliction, and the apostle John was imprisoned on the island of Patmos for his witness (2 Corinthians 12:7-10; Revelation 1:9). Tradition has it that the apostle Peter was crucified upside down.

Tim, it is difficult to make a case for the idea that faith in God equals a long, healthy, happy life. This is especially true today when so many illnesses are being caused by environmental pollution and the dumping of chemical wastes that contaminate land and water resources. Nevertheless, *generally speaking*, Christians who live by the teachings of our Lord do live longer, and they do live useful lives. Faith is an integral part of the wholeness of life they enjoy. But, thank God, *wholeness* and physical health are not synonymous. From a Christian perspective *wholeness is not necessarily* dependent upon our physical health (2 Corinthians 4:16-18). Some of those with the most profound faith and brightest spirits are Christians who have suffered much.

To sum up then, Tim, we just don't know why God chooses to perform miraculous cures in some cases but not in others. Genuine, mature faith is like that of Job. When he was suffering beyond endurance he refused to "curse God and die." Instead, he said: "Though he slay me, yet will I hope in Him" (Job 13:15). As Christians, however, we can be sure of this: God has promised us that death will not separate us from him—and that is good enough for me (Psalm 23:4; 139:1-18; Romans 8:35-39; John 14:25-27; 17:9-11).

Tim, I guess our difficulty is that we find it so hard to accept our human limitations. We want to know *everything*. While I think we should try to know and understand as much as we can, at best we can only see through a dim glass. But when we get "on the other side" we'll understand fully. Then we'll know, even as we are known by God (1 Corinthians 13:12). I didn't intend to get carried away, but the problem of evil—human suffering—is such a troublesome one.

While we believe God is all-powerful, we must accept the positive limitations he imposes on himself. He always acts in a manner consistent with his nature. We must not project the erratic attributes of man on him. God never acts in a capricious manner, even though it may appear that way at times. Just as we've often driven out of the storm clouds and the rain into bright, warm sunlight, so in our personal experience we pass from suffering and confusion to deliverance and understanding.

In addition, we must accept the fact that our freedom often limits God's activity. He doesn't coerce us. We are free to follow him or turn away. But even when we turn away he doesn't forsake us. Rather than viewing the noncoerciveness of God as a weakness, it is a strength. We both know parents who continue to try to run their children's lives even after they are grown. I can hear you saying, "I sure do, dad!"

Well, I'm trying to learn to let go. The fact that Steve, Debbi, and Susan came along before you was to your advantage. They taught me a lot about how to and how not to raise kids. Mom has done a better job of loving and not possessing than I. Anyway, I think this is what God does beautifully. He created and sustains each one of us, but he doesn't force himself on us—it's contrary to his nature.

I'd better stop at this point, Tim. In my next letter I'll share some more thoughts about God. But before I close, let me sum up what I've said about the nature and attributes of God. God *is;* and he has revealed himself. God not only reveals himself to us in the present in many ways, but in the past he revealed himself through his chosen people, Israel. Most fully and perfectly, God's nature has been revealed to us in Jesus Christ, our Savior and Lord. And we find the record of this historic revelation in the Bible that serves as our dependable guide for faith and human behavior.

We don't *project* "God out there." He *is* there and he reveals himself to us. While we refer to God as our heavenly Father, we realize that he is neither male nor female. But since God's revelation is an historical one, God and the witness of Scripture use anthropomorphic language to communicate the message of God to us. God is not only personal in his dealings with us, but he is an infinite, personal being. He is not only a God who is light, love, and truth, but he is also just. Tim, I realize, as you do, that there are many unanswerable questions in life. There is evil in the world, and too often the innocent do suffer for the guilty—Christ did this for us. It's difficult to square God's justice and love, as well as his omniscience and his omnipotence, with the evils that exist in the world. But, then, we are *only* human—finite creatures. And saying that, Tim, I'm not trying to cop out of a tight spot. Theodicy—the problem of reconciling the goodness of

God with the evil that exists in the world—has engaged some of the greatest minds in Christendom. But, nonetheless, it is a fact—we are only human. The finite cannot begin to fathom the mind of the infinite (Isaiah 55:8-9; Romans 11:33-34). All we can and must do is *trust* the omnipresent God. Someday we *will* understand. Meanwhile, we must not use our freedom to frustrate the will and purposes of God. But we must keep the faith and work with him to do the good.

Until later, Tim, God bless and keep you.

All my love,
Dad

God's Laws

Dear Tim,

There are more things I should have, perhaps, included in my last letter about the nature of God. One thing that I always felt was misleading was the way people talk about "natural law" or the "laws of nature." I know their intention is to identify what they think are regularities in nature, cause-effect relationships in the natural and physical world, as well as in the social world. However, this rules out *miracles*—what appear to be irregularities in nature and human experience. The tendency, especially of people in the sciences (oddly, more the social than the natural) is to rule out all that is not empirical (that which can be experienced by the physical senses).

From my perspective what is called natural law is man's discovery of part of the *laws*, or regular workings, *of God.* We often act like Columbus who "discovered America." The question is asked, "What did the Indian say to Columbus when he discovered America?" "Welcome!" So when modern people "discover" laws or principles of God's workings, there is no reason for boasting or pride. For God not only created the world, but also gave us the innate capacity to search things out and learn of his ways.

If the scientist defines truth as only that which can be empirically known, if he rules out the spiritual, intuitive, and psychosocial realities, he is guilty of distorting reality. He is giving only partial answers and half-truths. To get the complete picture, spiritual/psychological/social factors must be taken seriously. Most physicians and social scientists do recognize the inseparable link between human attitudes, dispositions, and feelings (love, hate, jealousy, envy) and physical and mental health. By doing this, they are able to develop more satisfactory prescriptions and programs for people. Therefore, I prefer to think of the various scholarly spheres as laying hold of aspects of the laws of God. When all the different ways of seeing and knowing are integrated into a "whole," mankind benefits as God intended.

The Christian, then, sees "natural law" as a part of God's law. Even the so-called miracle is a "natural happening" to God, since he established all the principles that operate in the world. From a Christian point of view, Tim, there is no such thing as "chance" or "luck." All events have meaning for God and for us. We may not always understand events and their relationship, but they do work into a pattern. If we are sensitive to God's leading, we can recognize his guiding hand (Proverbs 3:5-6; Psalm 25:8-10; 32:8; John 7:17; 16:13). Many times we can only see God's providential care and guidance as we review our past life.

I think, as I look back, of the time when your Uncle Mike was six and I was four years old. We lived in Merchantville, New Jersey, then. An old sinkhole was located at the edge of town, not far from our house. The hole was filled with water, and around the edge was a lot of nice junk with which we used to play. One morning Uncle Mike and I were playing near the edge and I slipped off the "pier" into the water.

Fortunately, Uncle Mike quickly grabbed me by the shirt and pulled me out. Then we went into our basement and I dried out my clothes by the coal furnace in the basement. Grandmom never knew. I've often thought, if Uncle Mike hadn't grabbed me, I'd be singing with the angels in heaven now!

I think, too, of the "chance" meeting I had with Dr. Stephen Paine (now President Emeritus of Houghton College) at Tenth United Presbyterian Church in Philadelphia. I was thinking of going back to college. I was planning to attend a fundamentalist "university" down South when one of my friends suggested that I speak with Dr. Paine about Houghton. As a result of my "chance" meeting with Dr. Paine, I went to Houghton. This was not only my intellectual salvation, but also my social salvation— I met your mother there. In retrospect I see in all of this, not chance or luck, but the providential hand of God. Now, I confess that not all events were good, nor could I fit them into a meaningful pattern at the time. But gradually I gained a clearer perspective on how God was working in my life. This was the patriarch Joseph's experience. His brothers sold him into slavery, but in the providence of God Joseph became a ruler in Egypt and was able to care for his people, Israel. He said to his brothers: "You plotted evil against me, but God turned it into good" (Genesis 50:20, TEV).

Tim, let me comment further about miracles. As I said, what we call a miracle is normal functioning for God, who works in a consistent manner. Many times he operates outside the pattern with which we are most familiar. But man, in his arrogance and pride, often plays *god* and rejects God and his ways because he cannot understand them. But as Christians, while we seek to learn, understand, and discover all we can, we humbly admit that we can't know all—his ways are not ours (Isaiah 55:8-9). He is infinite in wisdom and understanding; we aren't. There is really only one God, and we accept the fact that as sovereign ruler he is free to act when, where, and how he pleases. We rejoice that he has revealed all that he has to us. So I have faith that God is in control—that "miracles" are a natural part of his workings in the world.

Unfortunately (or fortunately), God hasn't chosen to "tell all." In the short run, Tim, I admit it's often difficult to see what he is doing. Sometimes we may feel that evil is triumphing over good. But if we take the long view of history, using biblical Israel as a microcosm of God's working in the world, we can see that in his own time the wicked have been overturned (Psalm 105; Amos 1:3—2:16; 1 Corinthians 1:20). God does liberate the oppressed and vindicate the righteous—if not in this world, then in the next. Death *is not* the end!

The hymn writer asks, "O where are kings and empires now?" Many of them are gone—if not the nation, the political regimes that ruled them. Many African countries are virtually free now from the old colonial powers that ruled over them until the last decade or so. Unfortunately, now many of them are being oppressed by their own political leaders. The oppressed have often become the oppressors, and the colonized are sometimes worse than the colonizers. Justice eventually does triumph and the oppressor and exploiter is overthrown. Nothing escapes the all-seeing eye of God (Hebrews 4:13). Fortunately, he is merciful. If he did not temper his justice with mercy and extend forgiveness, who would survive (Psalms 103:8; 117:2; 130:3)?

Nonetheless, I think that God's call for justice needs to be emphasized much more today than it is (Amos 5:24; Micah 6:8). Children don't profit from parents who refuse to discipline them. Instead, they grow up to be self-centered individuals who show little respect, and often contempt, for their parents and others. Likewise, Christians who are fed a diet of sentimentalism about God—love devoid of discipline and responsibility—acquire a distorted and false concept of God. As a result their lifestyle is often undisciplined, overindulgent, and irresponsible—harmful to themselves and others. Make no mistake; God does judge and discipline us (John 15:2; Hebrews 12:3-11).

When we had the Studebaker Lark station wagon (you were only two years old then), we were driving in West Philadelphia in heavy traffic. I was headed down a one-way street in the center lane in an unfamiliar neighborhood. Suddenly, I thought I saw a chance to turn left at an intersection. I had failed to see a car about to pass me in the left lane. Fortunately, we both stopped quickly and no one was injured. The moral of the story—you can't break traffic laws with impunity, not for long. Neither can we break the laws of God; they have a way of breaking us.

God, then, is righteous and just and he does judge us—here as well as hereafter. We do reap what *we* sow (Galatians 6:7). However, he provides ample opportunity for our forgiveness and renewal if we repent and turn from our sinful, ignorant, and self-destructive ways. This is what "the grace of God in Christ" is all about. More later.

In addition to judgment here and now, God will judge each of us at life's end. As the author of Hebrews says, "It is appointed for men to die once, and after that comes judgment" (9:27, RSV). Whether Christian or not, we still have to give account of our stewardship (2 Corinthians 5:10; Matthew 25:31-46; Luke 12:48). We will have to answer to God for the way we have used the talents and abilities he has given us (Matthew 25:14-30). Therefore, Tim, we ought to be careful about the kind and quality of the relationships we have within the family and with others in the community. While we are saved by grace, we still are obliged to live by the law of love (Mark 12:31; Romans 13:8; Galatians 5:13-14). This includes living justly, mercifully, and walking humbly with God and others (Micah 6:8). It also means attempting to do for others what we would like them to do for us, were we in their situation (Matthew 7:12). This not only means being loving by displaying forgiveness, but it also means being loving by being just—which is equally as important (Amos 5:24; Psalm 82:1-4; Deuteronomy 16:19-20).

Finally, Tim, God is Redeemer (Psalm 19:14; 2 Corinthians 5:18-21). He is one who delivers us from all that would enslave us. This does not mean that we dare disregard the laws of God and society, expecting him to deliver us. While he does forgive us when we repent of our sins and make restitution, we often still suffer for our mistakes. For example, the Studebaker Lark and the other fellow's car still had to be repaired and the bill paid. The alcoholic may quit drinking, but may still suffer from cirrhosis of the liver. The wrong decision—the selfish, self-advancing decision, whether on the part of the president of the United States or on our part—may have continued adverse consequences even though we repent (Numbers 14; Judges 16; 1 Kings 22). But having said this, God still delivers us in ever so many ways. Just as the magistrate, who shall remain nameless, delivered you from the penalty of a traffic violation that might have cost you your license for a few months, so God delivers us.

He has given us the Bible that contains sound principles to live by (Psalm 119:105). These are summed up in the Ten Commandments and the Sermon on the Mount. But in a real sense the Scriptures contain more than principles to live by; they focus on the great act of God's deliverance through Jesus Christ. When we come to know God in Christ and walk with him, we experience this deliverance—the abundant life in Christ (John 10:10b).

Tim, sometimes you'll hear of dramatic conversions from a life of gross immorality. Sometimes the convert exaggerates his or her perverseness, thinking that this "makes God look better." Young people who have been nurtured in a Christian family sometimes feel inferior to those who have experienced dramatic conversions. Since they have not rebelled to any great extent nor descended to the depths of the Prodigal, they feel as if they've missed out on something. But as Derek, a Welsh "prodigal" friend of Alan Jones who became a Christian in adulthood, said, "Those of you who have always believed and walked with Christ *really know* what the power of God is since it has kept you from falling into the depths that I have. Don't you ever feel that you have missed out on anything! I can assure you, you haven't!"

Finally, Tim, permit me a second "finally." God also delivers us from many otherwise oppressive and crippling experiences. Everyone—some more fortunate than others (and not because of any merit of their own)—can look back with gratitude and see God's hand of deliverance in life. Of course, we experienced the greatest act of deliverance when we opened our hearts to Christ.

So then, Tim, God is active in all of life. There is no *secular* sphere—*all of life is sacred.* What some call "natural law" is part of the "divine law" of God. Also, what we call "miracles" are merely part of God's normal workings in the lives of individuals, groups, and nations. As we seek to understand God's workings, we must recognize the part that the spiritual, the psychological, and the social, as well as the empirical or physical plays in our lives. From the Christian perspective there are no chance happenings—no such thing as luck. But through all events, God, in his providence, is working out his will and purposes for mankind and the world. While we may not understand what he's doing in the short run, in the long run we can often see his divine hand at work. Ultimately, in heaven, we'll understand. God is not only our Creator, but he is also our Judge. He judges us here, as well as hereafter. But, thank God, he is also our Redeemer and the one who sustains us. By his Holy Spirit who indwells us, he instructs and guides us through Scripture and in countless other ways.

In my next letter, Tim, I'll share some thoughts about Christ, our Savior and Lord. Until then, remember the family in your prayers. We pray for you all the time, that the Lord will continue to direct your life.

I love you,
Dad

God's Son and His Kingdom

Dear Tim,

In the last two letters I shared with you some thoughts about God. I concluded by saying that God is our Redeemer and that his great act of redemption took place in the *incarnation*—when God came in Jesus Christ, who gave his life to redeem us from the power of sin and death (Mark 10:45; 1 Peter 2:24; Hebrews 2:14-18). In this letter I want to share with you thoughts about Jesus Christ, our Savior and Lord. As Christians we believe in one God who reveals himself to us in three persons. The three, God the Father, God the Son, and God the Holy Spirit, form the Trinity, or the Godhead (2 Corinthians 13:14). The doctrine of the Trinity has engaged the greatest minds within the church. At best it is a difficult doctrine to explain and, historically, the church has insisted that the doctrine is crucial.

It is crucial because our salvation depends on it. By this I mean that *if* Jesus Christ is not "very God of very God" (as well as "very man of very man") *then* his sacrificial death could not atone for our sins. *If* he were merely a good man who died for principles he believed in, *then* his life could be redemptive for himself, but not for us. Both the New Testament and the church proclaim the good news that "God was in Christ, reconciling the world unto himself" (2 Corinthians 5:19). At God's appointed time he sent his Son into the world, who was incarnated in Jesus, a truly human being (Galatians 4:4-5; Philippians 2:5-7). Paul says that for a time the Son set aside his heavenly prerogatives in order to come to earth to assume the role of God's suffering servant to redeem us (Isaiah 53:1-12; 61:1-2a; Luke 4:18-19; Philippians 2:5-11; 2 Corinthians 9:8; Matthew 8:20; Acts 3:13-15; 4:23-31). So, Tim, while theologians and laymen have found the concept of "God in three persons" difficult to explain and fully understand, it is very important.

Likewise, the church has insisted on the New Testament teaching that Jesus was a *real* man. *If* he wasn't a real man, *then* his three-year ministry in which he wrestled with the forces of evil, as well as his agonizing death, were merely "role playing"—a pretense. I just can't buy that, Tim. Jesus was born of a woman (Galatians 4:4). He was a man of real flesh and blood (John 19:34). Jesus himself said after the resurrection, "Handle me, and see; for a spirit has not flesh and bones as you see that I have" (Luke 24:39, RSV). The author of Hebrews reminds us that Jesus was tempted in "every respect . . . as we are, yet without sin" (4:15, RSV). *If* Jesus were not truly human, *then* he was not tempted as we are. It is only because he was, and did not yield to temptation, that we are able to go to him and "receive mercy and find grace to help us in our time of need" (Hebrews 4:16).

Tim, when I was at Maryville College I spoke in chapel on one occasion on the humanity of Jesus Christ. In the course of my talk I suggested that Jesus probably noticed beautiful women and found them attractive, although not in any lustful, covetous way. After chapel, the chaplain took issue with me. He felt that our Lord was "above that." I disagreed. I was not saying that Jesus was lustful, but merely that he was a "normal male" who was in all points tempted like we are, yet without sin. After all, the sin does not lie in being tempted, but in yielding to it. Just as Jesus enjoyed the laughter of little children, grieved with those who mourned, compassionately healed the sick, in righteous anger reproved the hypocritical Pharisees, so he appreciated beauty when he saw it. The Apostles' and Nicene Creeds insist that Jesus was human. The Apostles' Creed says he was human: "He was *born* of the Virgin Mary, suffered under Pontius Pilate." And as the Nicene Creed says, he was God: "The only begotten Son of God, begotten of his Father before all worlds, God of God, Light of Light, very God of very God, begotten, not made, being of one substance with the Father."

Jesus Christ, therefore, we believe to be the God-man. As recorded in the Scriptures of the Old Testament, God promised that he would send the *Messiah,* which means "anointed deliverer." Kings and priests were all anointed leaders in Israel (Leviticus 8:12; 1 Samuel 16:13). The act of anointing with oil and the laying on of hands symbolized the transfer of divine power, as well as the commissioning to a special task. Moses, Aaron, and David are exalted in the Old Testament as the unique leaders (the latter two being anointed) who led the people of God. They occupied the offices of prophet, priest, and king respectively. Messianic ideas (ideas associated with the Messiah who was to come) grew up around all three offices (Deuteronomy 18:15-18; Matthew 21:11; 2 Samuel 7:8-17; Ezekiel 34:23-24; Matthew 21:9; Mark 12:35; Psalm 110:4; Hebrews 4:14-5:10).

In addition, Tim, in the Old Testament messianic ideas are associated with both the title Son of Man and that of the suffering servant of the Lord (Daniel 7:13-14; Isaiah 42:1-4;

49:1-6; 50:4-9; 52:13—53:12). Oddly, Son of Man is a heavenly messianic title because he descends from heaven to earth. However, whereas in the Old Testament his role was to wage war and defeat Israel's enemies, when Jesus employed it as a self-designation, he stripped it of any military connotations and blended it in with the ideas associated with the suffering servant of the Lord (Mark 10:45; Luke 4:18-21; Matthew 16:13-28; John 13:12-20). You're familiar with Isaiah 53 that talks about the servant who takes our sins upon himself. Ministers usually read from the servant passages of Isaiah in church around Good Friday each year, as well as at other times. In the Old Testament it seems to have a dual reference. It begins by referring to a "righteous remnant" or small holy group within Israel. But then the concept narrows down, referring to an individual who will come to redeem us. Certainly Jesus interpreted his role or mission to be that of the Son of Man who suffers as God's obedient servant (Mark 10:45).

One important fact that needs to be emphasized is that the Christian faith is a historical one. It is rooted in history. The Hebrews were God's chosen people. They had prophets among them who foretold that Christ would come. He was born in Bethlehem when Herod the Great ruled Judea, Quirinius was governor of Syria, and Caesar Augustus was emperor in Rome (Matthew 2:1; Luke 1:5; 2:1-7).

He came for a specific purpose—to do the will of God by living a redemptive life (John 4:34; 6:38; Mark 10:45). This includes both his teachings and his works, as well as his redemptive death. The resurrection and ascension of Jesus Christ from the dead bears witness to the fact that he accomplished his redemptive purpose (Luke 24:44-49).

Tim, if you'll read the birth narratives in Matthew and Luke you will find that in each case they predict the redemption that is to come in Christ. God tells the Virgin Mary, "You shall call his name Jesus, for he will save his people from their sins" (Matthew 1:21, RSV). Luke records various songs of praise that preceded and followed the birth of Jesus. All testify that he is the one who is bringing salvation (1:31-35; 46-55; 68-79; 2:22-38). If you look in the Gospel of John, Tim, you will find that the story of salvation begins in the Godhead (1:1-13). The eternal Word (the Son of God) is the light that comes into the world to offer eternal life to all who will receive him.

The purpose of Jesus' coming is made crystal clear in the Gospels. He came to usher in the kingdom of God. He said, "The time is fulfilled, and the kingdom of God is at hand; repent, and believe in the gospel" (Mark 1:14-15; Matthew 3:2, RSV). The word kingdom means rule or reign, so our Lord was saying that he came to usher in the rule of God. Obviously, he was not speaking about a literal, physical, geographical kingdom. He was talking about a *spiritual* one, one that we enter into by faith (John 18:36). It's internal, spiritual, and dynamic; he takes up his dwelling place in our hearts (Luke 17:20-21; John 7:37-39). When we yield to God through faith in Christ and obey his will, he rules in our hearts and lives.

Jeremiah, for example, predicted this. He said that in those days "I will put my law within them, and I will write it upon their hearts" (31:33, RSV). Ezekiel, likewise, speaks of the day when God will give to his people a "new heart" and a "new spirit" (36:26). The author of Hebrews witnesses to the establishment of this "new covenant" in Jesus Christ (8:1ff.; 10:11-13).

On one occasion the Pharisees asked when the kingdom of God would come, implying that it was a political, geographical entity. To this Jesus replied, "The kingdom of

God is not coming with signs to be observed . . . for behold, the kingdom of God is in the midst of you [within you]" (Luke 17:20-21, RSV). Furthermore, Tim, Jesus said unequivocally to Pilate, "My kingship is not of this world" (John 18:36, RSV). The many parables Jesus taught also substantiate the present reality of the kingdom or rule of God. In most cases he begins by saying "the kingdom of God" or "the kingdom of heaven" is like unto . . ." and then the parable illustrates and teaches some principle that we should live by *now*. (See, for example, Matthew 13:24, 31, 44, 45, 47.) Actually, Tim, the expressions "kingdom of God" and "kingdom of heaven" are synonymous terms. The Jews used "heaven" instead of "God" because they feared breaking the first commandment, "Thou shalt not take the name of the Lord thy God in vain." You will find that "heaven" is used in Matthew's Gospel, which was addressed primarily to the Jews. Of course, using a synonym for God doesn't preclude blasphemy, does it?

When Jesus came to redeem us, he was not merely role playing—or acting out a predetermined script. Jesus, the incarnate Son of God, came as a real man, as a prophet of God like Moses. In fact, the disciple Matthew presents Jesus as the *new Moses* who came with a *new law of God* (Matthew 5:7-48). You can see this in the way Matthew describes how Jesus delivered the Sermon on the Mount. He *sat down* when he taught as was the custom with Jewish teachers, but when he taught he did so with unusual authority (Matthew 7:28-29). He gives new insights into the old commandments. See especially Matthew 5:17, 27, 31, 33, 38, 43 where he elaborates on the social commands of Moses.

In true prophetic fashion Christ came to challenge the people to return to God. Luke records Jesus' visit to the synagogue where he read from Isaiah (61:1-2a):

> The Spirit of the Lord God is upon me, because the Lord has anointed me to bring good tidings to the afflicted; he has sent me to bind up the brokenhearted, to proclaim liberty to the captives, and the opening of the prison to those who are bound; to proclaim the year of the Lord's favor. And he closed the book, and gave it back to the attendant, and sat down.... And he began to say to them, "Today this scripture has been fulfilled in your hearing" (Luke 4:16-21).

Prophets preach judgment, as well as deliverance. Here Jesus is saying "no" to the oppressors and exploiters, and "yes" to the oppressed and exploited.

What was the good news that Jesus the prophet proclaimed which, if obeyed, would enrich our lives and all those around us? Basically it was this: to love God and to love our neighbor as ourselves (Mark 12:29-31). It's interesting that Jesus first mentioned loving God the Father with all our "heart, soul, and mind, and strength." We must get into a right relationship with him before we can begin to love ourselves and others. I said earlier that we are basically spiritual beings. When we live unworthily—abuse our bodies, dissipate our talents and gifts, act disrespectfully, inconsiderately, or harmfully toward others—it disrupts the rapport that exists between us and God. We have to begin by asking his forgiveness, for it is his love and moral code we have flaunted. When we sin, his name is degraded as well as ours.

The Old Testament emphasizes one unique difference between the Jews and others. When things went wrong politically or socially, unlike their "pagan" neighbors who attributed this to a weakness in their *deity*, the Jews assumed *they* were at fault. The prophets called them to turn from their evil ways and things would be made right (2 Chronicles 7:14; Ezekiel 18:19-20). This is a basic assumption within our faith; we, not God, bear primary responsibility for what goes wrong in our lives (Jeremiah 18:1-10). Salvation, wholeness, therefore, must begin by our loving God, and we do this by obeying his commands.

In addition to loving God, we must love our neighbor as we love ourselves. As Christians who have been forgiven, we can like ourselves. We show our love for ourselves by forgiving our failings and shortcomings, as God in Christ has forgiven us. Jesus asks us to do the same for others—be as forgiving, loving, and supportive as God is with us (Matthew 18:23-35; Ephesians 4:32). Just as God did not return evil for our evil, but loved us—"his enemies"—so we must love others. This is hard to do at times, but if we constantly remind ourselves that this is what God does for us, we can do no other. This is why I think the "peace" churches such as the Mennonites, which take a pacifist stand, are sound in their basic doctrine (Matthew 5:38-48; 26:52).

The twofold command, love God and neighbor, cannot really be separated. How can one love God and not love his children? How can one love a neighbor who is a child of God and not love the Father (1 John 4:19-21; James 2:15-17)?

Jesus incurred the wrath of the Jewish establishment of his day because he insisted on loving *all* persons equally. It made no difference to him if a person were Gentile, Samaritan, female or male, young or old, leper or lame, common or "holy," poor or rich. Because he healed all, because he received all, the legalistic Jews who had neatly defined and packaged God were angry with Jesus (Matthew 9:10-13; Luke 19:7). They saw him as a troublemaker who was interpreting the nature of God, and mankind's responsibility to God, in a way that was different from theirs. They faced two options: either change their concepts and ways, or get rid of him. Tim, it's really difficult to change one's ways—to give up cherished ideas and prejudices. But if we're going to follow Jesus we have to let the "new wine" of the gospel ferment and expand in our lives, driving out false ideas and prejudices (Mark 2:22).

In addition to his teaching about love, a second basic teaching of Jesus involves forgiveness. Not only does God forgive the penitent, but he expects us to do the same. Jesus illustrated this in his parable of the unforgiving servant (Matthew 18:23-35). A man who owed his king several million dollars was forgiven after he pleaded for mercy because there was no way he could get that kind of money to pay his debt. The man who was forgiven, however, turned right around and had a fellow servant thrown in prison because he could not pay the few dollars he owed him. When word got back to the king, he threw the unforgiving servant in jail. Jesus added, "So also my heavenly Father will do to every one of you, if you do not forgive your brother from your heart" (Matthew 18:35).

Forgiveness, then, is conditional on our forgiveness of others. When we pray the Lord's Prayer we affirm this truth—"forgive us our debts (obligations/sins), *as we forgive our debtors*" (those who are obligated to us—who have wronged us). Sometimes, however, people are not penitent. What do you do then? Well, our Lord said, "If your brother sins, rebuke him, and if he repents, forgive him" (Luke 17:3; Matthew 18:15-17). We should always have a forgiving attitude, but if a person won't repent, forgiveness ought not to be extended. Otherwise, you'd be "casting your pearls before swine." Tim, to a great extent, this explains the steady rise in juvenile delinquency. The delinquent is treated as if "the darling didn't do anything at all," or his delinquent act is attributed to "the poor kid's background." Consequently he gets off scott free and then mocks the law. He doesn't respect the law or the authorities because *he knows* he did something wrong. He figures that if they are that stupid and he can get away with it, he'll keep working the system.

God has a forgiving attitude toward us. He gave his Son to redeem us. Jesus said from the cross, "Father, forgive them; for they know not what they do" (Luke 23:34, RSV). But unless you and I repent and ask for forgiveness, the transaction cannot be completed. This is the way it is with us when we offend one another. Reconciliation is not complete until the offending party changes his attitude or turns himself around. That is what repentance means.

Jesus tells us that if we know someone has a gripe or grievance with us, we should go and try to make it right (Matthew 5:23-24). Likewise, if we have a grievance against anyone, our Lord tells us to take the initiative and seek to be reconciled (Matthew 18:15-17).

But, Tim, we've got to watch out for self-righteousness. The Pharisees were good at this and, unfortunately, there's a "Pharisee" in each one of us. They were the ones who brought *the woman* whom they had caught in the act of adultery to Jesus. Notice, they didn't bring *the man*, but the woman! They reminded Jesus that according to the law of Moses she should be stoned. But Jesus said the one who was without sin should cast the first stone. They all walked away—every last one (John 8:1-11). Likewise, in the Sermon on the Mount, Jesus said that to entertain lustful thoughts is to commit adultery in one's heart (Matthew 5:27-28). Jesus cautions us to be careful about finding fault, because God will judge us with the same standard we apply to others (Matthew 7:1-5). Obviously, we have to make judgments about people and situations, but we must always do it with care.

Let me close with this paradoxical thought. While we are

instructed to forgive seventy times seven (as often as one repents), this doesn't mean that when forgiven we will not be punished or disciplined. You wouldn't turn a repentant rapist out on the street or put him to work in a girl's juvenile center, would you? You wouldn't keep a known kleptomaniac or arsonist in a position where he could be tempted to rob or set fires, would you? God forgives the genuine penitent, and so should we. But we should also do for him what we would want someone to do for us. If a person has a unique problem, we should redirect his life and place him in a position and situation where he can get help. Tim, my point is that we must always be careful, when we interpret our Lord's teachings, that we do not do it in isolation. Specific concepts must always be related to others, such as love and justice.

This is enough for now. I'll pick up on some of the teachings of Jesus in my next letter. But let me sum up what I've said about our Lord so far.

Jesus Christ was not only truly human, but also truly divine. As a man he was tempted but he resisted all temptation to sin. He was completely obedient to the will of God, and thereby overcame the powers of evil. Jesus was God's anointed one, the Messiah. He embodied the roles of prophet, priest, and king. He was not only the Son of Man from heaven, but he was also God's obedient suffering servant.

Jesus' life—his work and words and his vicarious death— were all redemptive. God authenticated Christ's redemptive work when he raised Jesus from the dead and received him into heaven, seating him at the place of honor at his right hand (Hebrews 1:3-4; Philippians 2:9). Jesus came preaching the good news of the coming kingdom or rule of God. His kingdom is a spiritual one that we enter through repentance and faith. In Christ God offers us present deliverance from sin and its power. God ushered in the new covenant, thus fulfilling Old Testament prophecy.

Our Lord taught us that we must love God, put him first, and that we must also love our neighbor as ourselves. Just as he forgives us, so we must forgive one another. Forgiveness, however, does not always stop or eliminate the consequences of our words and actions. Therefore, it's important to walk close to Christ.

Take good care of yourself, Tim. If you need anything, be sure to let us know.

All my love,
Dad

Humility, Good Works, and Prayer

Dear Tim,

When I was attending Houghton College I had a good friend, Bill. He is now a serious scholar, a historian, and an Episcopal clergyman. Back then Bill was quite a cutup. He used to say jokingly, "Have you read my latest book, *Humility, and How I Attained It?*" Humility is one of those virtues one is not aware of having. When you think you've got it, you've lost it!

Humility not only means that we should not have an exaggerated opinion of our own importance, but it also means that we esteem others better than ourselves (Romans 12:3; Philippians 2:3). It means that after we've done all that we can do for others, and God, we think of it only as our common duty (Luke 17:10).

Even if we have special gifts, and a list of accomplishments, there really isn't any room for boasting. For as the apostle Paul said, "What do you have that you did not receive? And if you did receive it, why do you boast as though you did not?" (1 Corinthians 4:7).

I like the card you sent mom on Mother's Day, Tim.

> You might as well admit it, mother,
> I'm terrific and as smart as can be!
> It's clearly a case of heredity!
> Happy Mother's Day.

It reminded me of the dean's daughter at Lock Haven State College who came home exclaiming over her high IQ. Her dad said, "You don't need to think you had anything to do with it!"

In Jesus' teachings he emphasizes the fact that we must humble ourselves and become as little children (Matthew 18:1-4)—not childish, but childlike in faith and trust. This same idea is conveyed in the Beatitudes, "Blessed are the poor in spirit" and "Blessed are the meek" (Matthew 5:3, 5). If we are ready to acknowledge our need, our inadequacy, and submit to God, then we shall indeed inherit "the kingdom" and "the earth." Here again, Tim, our Lord is talking about the blessings of his rule in our hearts now.

Those who arrogantly exalt themselves shall be brought low (Matthew 23:12). Quite often the high-and-mighty are brought low in this life, but if they appear to escape they will certainly be justly rewarded in the next (Luke 16:19-31; James 5:1). Our Lord tells us that if we are filled with pride and boasting, we have already received our reward. We will not inherit the kingdom in the life to come (Matthew 6:2; James 4:6).

Jesus' classic parable about the need for humility is that of the two men who went into the temple to pray—one a Pharisee and the other a tax collector (Luke 18:9-14). From a Pharisee's point of view, Tim, tax collector and Sinner with a capital "S" were synonymous. The Pharisee, on the other hand, typifies self-righteous religionists who look down their noses at others. The Pharisee told God how virtuous he was in comparison with others, such as *that* sinner—the tax collector. As I mentioned before, by comparison, we can always find someone worse than ourselves. However, God doesn't measure us against one another, but by his righteous standard. In his sight none of us is righteous (Romans 3:10). In essence, Jesus said the Pharisee condemned himself by his haughty, self-righteous attitude. But the "tax collector" found mercy in God's sight and went away justified because he was willing to humble himself and admit his sinfulness.

Our Lord demonstrated the kind of humility we should display by his life. Although he was God incarnate, yet he performed the servant's role when he washed his disciples' feet in the upper room where they shared the Feast of the Passover (John 13:1-20). And he commanded us to act out the servant role in our relationship with one another in the fellowship of the church (13:14-15). Many of the peace churches observe this ordinance along with the Lord's supper, and rightly so. The act of foot washing symbolizes humility and reminds us of our Lord's example. I know it doesn't guarantee an attitude of humility—but neither does the act of baptism or the Lord's supper guarantee the genuine experience of the participant.

Another emphasis of our Lord's teaching which is crucial is service, or doing good. The expression "do-gooder" is often used as an epithet by people who object to individuals who uncover corruption and inefficiency. Many times it identifies individuals who are legalistic and neurotically obsessed with dotting every "i" and crossing every "t"—the kind of person who would turn his mother over to the police if she kept a dime she found in a coin return box in a telephone booth. Nonetheless, as Christians we should be doers of good.

Actually, Tim, one of the characteristics of Jesus' ministry that the disciples emphasized was that he went about *doing good* (Acts 10:38). Jesus commanded us to do good works so that others will glorify God (Matthew 5:15; John 15:8). In fact, Jesus insists that God's way to status is through playing the servant role, even as our Lord did. Jesus said that Gentiles (or pagans) think one is great if he "lords it over others." But he said that in the Christian community greatness ought to be determined by service—or servanthood (Mark 10:42-44). Again Jesus set the example, "For the Son of man also came not to be served but to serve, and to give his life as a ransom for many" (Mark 10:45, RSV).

Self-denial is an aspect of servanthood. Tim, we're living through a period in which some psychologists are emphasizing that it's bad for one to play a servant role. They would have us believe that deferring to others, denying ourselves for the sake of others, is counterproductive—even foolish. One occasionally hears of churches that are conducting courses on self-assertiveness, liberation, and the like. These concepts are often expressed in a manner that is contrary to Scripture. While humility doesn't mean becoming a doormat and letting people walk all over you, it can't be divorced from mutual submission and sacrificial service (Galatians 5:13; Ephesians 5:21; Romans 14:19; 15:1-2; 1 Corinthians 10:24). Jesus *did* say that we must deny our selfish desires and put the rule of the kingdom first: "Seek ye first the kingdom of God ..." (Matthew 6:33, KJV). When we put ourselves first—and try to save our lives—we lose them (Mark 8:35 ff). The cross is for crucifixion. Jesus said that we should put to death our selfish desires. By doing this we find the happiness we seek. Tim, happiness is a by-product of service. I think your brother and sisters and mother demonstrate this well. So do many in the various churches and communities we have lived in.

Jesus' teachings about self-denial weren't readily accepted

in his day. Likewise, Christians today often fail to display a loving acceptance of *all* people. Each of us needs to work actively at keeping our personal lives in order. This means serving our Lord in whatever ways we can. It is true that no matter how hard we try, we won't be able to achieve perfection, nor will we be able to please everyone. But Christ commands us to love others anyway—just as he loves us, even when we don't deserve it (Romans 5:8; John 15:12-17; Matthew 5:43-48).

Still another cluster of Jesus' teachings centers on prayer. Tim, I've stopped trying to figure out how prayer works; I just pray. It's natural to talk to God the Father, just as we talk things over with each other and with friends. Jesus commanded us to pray for health and strength and not to lose heart (Luke 18:1). In one parable there was a rascal who served as a judge. A widow went to him with a grievance, but he didn't want to be bothered. However, she was so persistent that he acted on her behalf just to get her off his back (Luke 18:2-5). Jesus then says that God is not like an unscrupulous judge. He is just and compassionate and he will answer our requests (Luke 18:6-7).

Again, Tim, the important ingredient is faith. "Whoever would draw near to God must believe that he exists and that he rewards those who seek him" (Hebrews 11:6, RSV). We must ask, seek, and knock—actively share with God our hopes and aspirations, our intercessions, and our thankfulness (Luke 11:9). If your mother and I provide for you and your brother and sisters when you have a need, how much more will God? (Luke 11:1-13).

Tim, although our Lord says that we ought to pray and that he will grant us our requests if we pray in his name and in accordance with his will, a word of caution is needed (Mark 12:2-4; Matthew 21:22; Luke 18:1; John 14:12-14;

16:23-24; 1 John 5:14). Not all our petitions are necessarily in accordance with his will. Also, before many prayers can be answered we must meet the conditions laid down in Scripture. At some of our early morning prayer meetings when I was attending Houghton College, students would ask the Lord to help them with exams, but they didn't read, review, or study as much as they should have. A lot of good it did to pray. While the Lord created the world out of nothing, so far as I know he only helps us recall and utilize in an examination material we have taken the time to learn. Ordinarily, conditions must be met. God ordains *means* (study), as well as *ends* (success in exams).

Furthermore, Tim, there is a time to pray and a time not to. A college friend, Myron Bromley, is a missionary in New Guinea. He and his colleagues were confronted by a couple of cannibals. Myron's friend fell on his knees to pray. Myron said, "This is no time to pray" (physically assume the position), and with a few coins or trinkets he managed to get away safely. Also, there are times when prayer must be accompanied with work. When you kids were sick, mom and I prayed, but we also bathed you when you had a high fever and gave you medication. While we should always be in an attitude of prayer, God expects us to answer many of our prayers ourselves. As Paul said, "For each man will have to bear his own load," as well as bear the burdens of others (Galatians 6:5, RSV).

Also, Tim, many times our petitions are out of harmony with God's will and the answer he gives is *no*! That is a legitimate answer! Remember our Lord's prayer that God deliver him from the cross. God's answer was no (Mark 14:36). Sometimes we've done our best, we've met the conditions, but things still don't work out for us. Then we get upset and fret and say, "Man, I don't know why I wasn't able to attain

Dear Tim

that goal." Sometimes God has other plans for us. Of course we know it is out of the will of God. But we live to regret it (Psalm 106:13-15). Nevertheless, Tim, even when we've made a mistake—and forced God's hand, as it were—if we reconcile ourselves with God, he will make things work together for good.

But let's get back to a crucial element in Jesus' teaching, namely, that all are welcome in his presence. He rejects no one, not even the sinner—because that's all of us, isn't it? Of course we must be penitent (Isaiah 55:6-7; Luke 15:17-24; 18:9-14). That is why he cleansed the Jerusalem temple. The Jews set up their animal sales and money changing in the Gentile Court of the Jerusalem temple. This meant the Gentiles could not enter the temple to worship. Jesus drove out the money changers and sellers of animals, so that the Gentiles could enter to worship God (Mark 11:15-19). By his action he said, "Let all God's children approach him." But the Pharisees couldn't take this radical change. Unlike Jonah who ran away from God's command, the Pharisees tried to silence God's messenger.

Now sometimes you'll hear people say, "The only prayer God hears from the sinner is a prayer of repentance." That is patently false. Obviously, we cannot be in full fellowship with God if we "cherish iniquity" in our hearts (Psalm 66:18). But as I mentioned, we're all sinners. We can talk to him at any time. Naturally, he wishes us to repent and confess our sins. But while we're coming around to full fellowship, he is there. He cares and wants us to stay in touch. A human analogy is helpful here. When you or I offended one another, sometimes we used to stew awhile before we worked it out, but we still communicated about other things. It only stands to reason that God is even more anxious to keep in touch. So, Tim, always talk things over with God, even when you don't feel like it, even when you think he's been unfair. After a period of prayer and meditation you'll come around to understanding God's will more clearly—or to accept the mystery involved in God's presence, to accept your lack of understanding. Prayer is not an instrument to manipulate or change God's mind, but to bring our mind around to his perspective—or as Paul might put it, it is a way of "renewing the mind" (Romans 12:2; Philippians 2:5-11).

I haven't said much about the Lord's Prayer, the model prayer Jesus gave to his disciples. It begins with adoration and praise, continues with petitions for God's rule to come, for life's necessities (bread), for forgiveness and deliverance from temptation, and it concludes acknowledging that ultimately every good thing comes from God's gracious hand (Matthew 6:9-13). Notice, Tim, it's a corporate prayer. We are not only to pray for ourselves but for all mankind.

By way of summary, Tim, our Lord wants us to be humble and not to think that we are better than others. Remember, whatever gifts and abilities we have we received from God, mediated to us through both our parents and others—to whom we're heavily indebted. But our primary role model is Jesus, not the Pharisee. Jesus assumed the role of a servant. As Christians we measure greatness by his rule, by how much of a servant role we assume. An aspect of servanthood is self-denial. Despite the emphasis today on assertiveness and demanding our rights, the example of the upper room was one of servanthood, self-denial, and mutual submission. Humility and self-denial lead to an attitude and atmosphere of mutual acceptance and harmonious cooperation in relationships, Tim. And this, standing in marked contrast to the attitudes and values of the world, is what we need today.

Our Lord demonstrated, by his example, the fact that prayer is our life breath. Jesus said that we should always pray and not lose heart. We pray, though, not to change God's mind, but to understand the mind of God—his will for us. We also pray to give thanks, to praise, and to intercede for others. God is eager to answer our prayers. He never turns anyone away from his presence. However, we must be penitent, humble, and receptive to his will. Remember, Tim, God answers *no*, and *wait awhile*, just as he answers yes. So keep in touch with him through continuous prayer, as I am sure you do. Let us always pray for one another, the family, and all peoples—that God will draw us closer and closer to himself and thereby closer to one another.

There are many other teachings of our Lord that I could share with you, but I'll stop with these. When I write my next letter, dealing with Jesus as Messiah, I'll touch on some others.

Take care of yourself.

> Love you, Tim, looking forward to
> seeing you,
> Dad

The Claims of Christ

Dear Tim,

In a previous letter I mentioned that Jesus came preaching, "Repent, for the kingdom of heaven (God) is near" (Matthew 3:2). As God's anointed deliverer, or Messiah, Jesus came to teach, work wonders (miracles of healing and exorcisms), and die to redeem us. His messiahship was confirmed by the resurrection (Matthew 4:23; Acts 2:36; Romans 1:4; 1 Peter 1:3-5).

Let me mention the things that point to his messiahship, and to the fact that Jesus is the Son of God. Many apologists (individuals who defend the gospel and Christ against those who would attack it and deny Christ's divinity) emphasize that when you look at the life of Christ you are left with only two choices. One either confesses with Thomas that Jesus is "My Lord and my God" or rejects him as an imposter who made false claims of divinity—a phony. (John 20:28; 12:44-50; Mark 6:3; 14:61-65). There really isn't any middle ground. You can't say, "I like some of his teachings, but I reject his claim to divinity." If he lied about that, how can you put any faith in his teachings?

The first thing that points to Jesus' messiahship occurred

at his baptism when God spoke from heaven, "Thou art my beloved Son; with thee I am well pleased." (Mark 1:11, RSV). In addition, at his baptism Jesus received the fullness of the Holy Spirit (Mark 1:10-11). Empowered by the Spirit, Jesus resisted the temptations of the devil in the wilderness, and then embarked on his public ministry (Mark 1:12-15; Matthew 4:1-17).

Second, his power to heal the sick, to raise the dead, and to cast out demons all point to the fact that he was divine (Mark 1:21-28, 34, 39, 40-41). When John the Baptist was in prison, he sent messengers to ask Jesus if he was the Messiah. Jesus replied by quoting from Isaiah: "Go and tell John what you hear and see: the blind receive their sight and the lame walk, lepers are cleansed and the deaf hear, and the dead are raised up, and the poor have good news preached to them" (Matthew 11:4-5; Isaiah 35:5-6, RSV). In essence, our Lord was saying that messianic prophesies are being fulfilled. I won't dwell on Jesus' miracles, since I wrote about them earlier. However, Tim, let me make this point. Often unbelievers, and some believers, have attempted to rationalize miracles in various ways—to explain them away. Their complaint is that they don't fit into a neat, naturalistic concept of things. My answer is that Jesus was no ordinary person; he was *the* man, God incarnate. If we believe in the incarnation—that God was in Christ—Jesus' miracles pose no problem. In fact, they serve as an authentication of his messiahship (John 3:12; 10:41; Acts 2:22).

Third, Jesus forgave sins (Mark 2:6; 10-11; Luke 7:48). As his critics said, only God can forgive sins. Jesus, therefore, assumed the prerogative of God.

Fourth, he had power to control the elements of nature. He spoke and the fierce winds ceased and the stormy waves became calm (Mark 4:35-41).

Fifth, he claimed to be Lord of institutions, or social structures. He said, "For the Son of Man is Lord of the Sabbath" (Matthew 12:8). His foes became angry with him because he healed the sick and worked on the Sabbath (12:1-14). But Jesus believed that people are more important than institutions. Unfortunately, Tim, people then were sacrificed to institutions even as they are today.

Tim, when you put these five things together, they're quite impressive. Jesus himself gave three messianic signs. The first sign was his miracles which I have already mentioned. The two others were the cleansing of the temple and the Passover meal.

The cleansing of the temple symbolized several things, Tim. First, by this act Jesus was saying that priests and sacrifices were no longer necessary to worship God. You can go directly to God—Christ has opened the way (Mark 15:38; John 2:19-21; 1 Timothy 2:5). This truth is one of the basic truths of the Protestant Reformation, one which is being increasingly embraced by Roman Catholics also.

Second, as I mentioned in my last letter, when Jesus drove the animals and the money changers out of the Gentile Court of the temple, he was inviting the Gentiles in to worship God. He was saying that the concept of "chosen people" has changed. The chosen people are no longer the Jews, per se, but all those who have faith and obey his word (Romans 2:25-29; Galatians 5:6; 6:15; Ephesians 2:14-18; 3:3; Colossians 2:11-13). As Jesus said earlier, where you worship is not important, nor who you are—that is, what nationality you are. God is Spirit and those who worship him must worship in Spirit and truth (John 4:24). "Come to me, all who labor and are heavy laden; and I will give you rest" (Matthew 11:28, RSV). "Him who comes to me I will not cast out" (John 6:37, RSV).

John's Gospel makes it even clearer. When Jesus cleansed the temple, the Jews wanted to know by what sign or by whose authority he cleansed it. He replied, "Destroy this temple, and in three days I will raise it up" (John 2:19, RSV). John adds from a post-resurrection perspective that Jesus was speaking of the temple of his body (1:21). Jesus, therefore, becomes the *door* for all who would be reconciled to the Father (John 10:7-9).

The third messianic sign was the Passover meal. When Jesus broke the bread and poured out the wine into the cup, he passed them to his disciples and said, "Take; this is my body.... This is my blood of the covenant, which is poured out for many" (Mark 14:22-25, RSV). The broken bread and poured out wine symbolized the sacrifice he was soon to make for them and us.

There is a lot more I could share with you about Jesus, but I think these things help you to see that he was indeed the Son of God. His teachings were prophetic (he spoke the Word of God plainly) and his works were priestly (compassionate and comforting). But the act that identifies him as our Savior is his voluntary death on our behalf. No one forced him to offer his life; he did it voluntarily. Like a good shepherd who gives his life for his sheep, he willingly gave his life for us (John 10:11-18). He saw death coming, as he graphically portrayed for his disciples in the parable of the vineyard and in his comments at the Last Supper (Mark 12:1-12; 14:22-25).

But he had also told his disciples of his impending death earlier, about halfway through his ministry. When he came to a place called Caesarea Philippi, Jesus asked them " 'Who do you say that I am?' Peter answered him, 'You are the Christ' " (Mark 8:27-29, RSV). After this great confession, which Peter probably spoke for all the disciples,

Jesus began to tell them that he would be killed, but he would rise again (Mark 8:30-32).

Tim, you're familiar with the crucifixion story—the agony and the accompanying last words. When Jesus uttered the words, "It is finished," he was referring primarily to the fact that he had fulfilled his redemptive ministry (John 19:30). From a Christian theological perspective, it wasn't only the Jews and the Romans who were involved in the crucifixion; it was *all* the forces of evil—human and demonic. My PhD dissertation is devoted wholly to this theme. What I show there is that the forces of evil were completely routed and stripped of their power by the crucifixion, resurrection, and ascension. Scriptures such as 1 Corinthians 2:8-10; Colossians 2:15; and Hebrews 2:14-18 substantiate this.

And, Tim, the early church saw the cross as the decisive battleground, not some future battle at Armageddon. That is why the Roman Catholics consider Jesus on the cross as their symbol of victory. Of course the resurrection followed, thereby authenticating that Christ had conquered the forces of evil on the cross.

But the resurrection came as a joyful surprise to the disciples. For they had thought "the jig was up"—that it was all finished. As the two on the road to Emmaus lamented, "But we had hoped that he was the one to redeem Israel" (Luke 24:21, RSV). Even Peter and his friends had decided to go back to fishing (John 21:3). And the faithful women went to the tomb to prepare the body for a proper Jewish burial (Mark 16:1). So, Tim, when Jesus revealed himself to his followers they *did not* expect him to rise again from the dead. It was not a case of "wishing and making it so," certainly not with all the evidence recorded. Perhaps *one* might see a "vision," but not *all* of them. The resurrected Christ appeared to Mary Magdalene and her female companions

(Matthew 28:1-10; John 21:11-18), twice to the disciple band (28:16-17; John 20:19-29), to the two on the Emmaus road (Luke 24:36-43), to doubting Thomas (John 20:24-29), and to Simon Peter (John 21). In 1 Corinthians Paul mentions other appearances: "to over five hundred brethren at one time, to James, and to Paul" (15:5-8).

After the resurrection Jesus appeared to his disciples and taught them the meaning and significance of his life, death, and resurrection. Luke is the basic source here. You might be surprised as you read Luke 24:44-49, Tim. Jesus says that *now*, as a result of his sacrificial death and triumphant resurrection, *repentance* and *forgiveness* of sins should be preached in his name to all nations. He didn't say to go out and preach hellfire and damnation. The gospel is the good news of salvation—deliverance. It is a present salvation, not an otherworldly message, but one for us as we live now. Of course, salvation includes a future blessed hope, but it is Christ in us *now* that guarantees the future (Colossians 1:27).

Most of the Jews, as well as most non-Jews, believed in life beyond the grave (John 11:24; Matthew 22:23-33). The good news of the gospel is that we become the inheritors of the eternal quality of life right here and now (John 3:18; 11:25-26; Romans 8:11; Ephesians 2:1, 5). This is what the early Christians preached—present deliverance from the power of sin. They didn't dwell on heaven out there. Of course we believe that when we die we continue to live in God's presence in another dimension—heaven (1 Corinthians 15:35-58; 2 Corinthians 5:1-5; Philippians 1:21-23). But our faith and hope for the future is based on the fact of our redemption in Christ *(past)*, and our *present* experience (Christ dwelling within).

When you look back from this side of the resurrection, you can see the "present emphasis" of salvation throughout the New Testament. Just let me mention a few places where you find this in the Sermon on the Mount: the Beatitudes all have both a present emphasis and a promise of immediate reward to the believer; the Lord's Prayer is present-oriented; the expressions "in heaven" in Matthew 5:12 and 6:20 refer to God and have a present emphasis; and, finally, the two ways of building—on rock or sand—refer to present blessings or judgment to the obedient and disobedient, respectively (Matthew 5—7).

Parables such as the prodigal son clearly state that the "lost *is* found" and the "dead *is* alive" (Luke 15:11-32). Zacchaeus received salvation "today" (Luke 19:1-10). You also see the present emphasis in John's Gospel most clearly where he states that if you believe (present tense) you have eternal life, but if you don't, you're condemned already—it's not something that happens to you out there (John 3:18). When you turn to the book of Acts and the Epistles you also find it unequivocally stated. For example, "Repent, and be baptized every one of you in the name of Jesus Christ for the forgiveness of your sins; and you shall receive the gift of the Holy Spirit" (Acts 2:38, RSV; see also 10:43; 13:38-39; 16:30-31). Paul says that those who are spiritually dead are made alive through repentance and faith in Jesus (Ephesians 2:1). This new life is something we experience now, freely (Ephesians 2:8-9; 2 Corinthians 5:17; Romans 8:1-11).

Finally, Tim, after our risen Lord spent some time with his disciples, instructing them, he ascended into heaven. Before he did, however, he commissioned them to go and make disciples of all peoples (Matthew 28:19-30). They were not to be overly preoccupied with the "end"—the return of Christ. They were to begin in Jerusalem and move out into Judea, Samaria, and the uttermost parts of the earth, sharing the good news (Acts 1:6-11).

So, Tim, the evidence supporting the fact that Jesus is the Messiah is overwhelming. There are only two logical responses we can make to the claims of Christ. Either accept him as Lord and Savior or reject him as an imposter—a deceiver. God confirmed Jesus' messiahship on various occasions: at Jesus' baptism, by his miracles, when he forgave sins, by his lordship over human institutions, when he cleansed the temple, and by his witness at the Passover meal. We confess with Peter and Thomas, "You [Jesus] are the Christ, the Son of the living God" (Matthew 16:16). You are "my Lord and my God!" (John 20:28).

Of course it was his voluntary, vicarious death that really brings us to our knees, confessing him as Savior and Lord. The cross is the symbol of our salvation, for it was there that Christ decisively defeated the devil and his demonic powers. The resurrection and ascension witness to the fact that God accepted the sacrifice of Christ's finished work on the cross. He commissioned his apostles to go forth proclaiming *present* deliverance and forgiveness, and to offer the free gift of the Holy Spirit to empower us to live the abundant life. The Gospels all testify to these truths, as do the other New Testament books. The good news of the gospel is not an offer of "pie in the sky by and by." It is for us today, right here where we live—where we hurt and need.

I'll close this letter now, Tim, quite aware that there is so much more that could and should be said about our Lord.

Until the next time, Tim, take care. The Lord bless and keep you. Continue your witness for Christ.

With all my love,
Dad

The Holy Spirit and His Work

Dear Tim,

So far I've written about God and our Lord Jesus Christ. Now I want to share some thoughts about the Holy Spirit. Generally speaking we associate God the Father with the creation and sustenance of all things (Genesis 1:1; John 1:1-3; Colossians 1:15-20). We also associate God with redemption and with judgment (Exodus 6:6; Psalms 77:15; 103:4; 106:10; Isaiah 43:1, Psalms 7:11; 10:17-18; Isaiah 2:4; Ecclesiastes 3:17; Jeremiah 11:20; Acts 17:31; 1 Peter 1:17). God, who gave his Son to redeem us, will someday judge us all by Christ (Matthew 25:31-46; Romans 2:15-16; 2 Corinthians 5:10).

God, in Christ, fully experienced our humanity and through his life and work revealed his essential nature, or attributes, to us (John 1:14; 14:8-9; Galatians 4:4; Philippians 2:5-9). Christ reveals God as our loving Father who redeems us and with the Son sends the Holy Spirit to minister to us and through us (John 3:16; 14:26; 15:26; 16:7-15).

The Holy Spirit, the third person of the Trinity, is God and Christ active in man and the world today. In the Bible you'll find the Holy Spirit, God's Spirit, the Spirit of God, the Spirit of Christ, and Christ's Spirit all used interchangeably. The Holy Spirit is not a nondescript force. Nor is he merely the "spirit" of God with a small *s*, as I might refer to my mother's continued influence in my life long after her death. The Holy Spirit is a person of the Godhead. Just as the Son has existed from all eternity, so has the Holy Spirit. The Holy Spirit is mentioned in Genesis 1:2 and throughout the Scriptures. He speaks to all persons, believers and nonbelievers alike (Genesis 20:3; Ezra 1:1; Isaiah 45:1; Acts 7:51; 1 Thessalonians 5:19). We are able to profess faith in Jesus only because the Spirit has enabled us to see our need, has opened our spiritual eyes to understand the gospel, and has led us to embrace Christ as Savior and Lord (2 Corinthians 3:12-18; 1 John 4:2). As Paul said, "No one can say 'Jesus is Lord' except by the Holy Spirit" (1 Corinthians 12:3, RSV).

God's Spirit is continually working with men and women to bring them to salvation. But I'm getting ahead of myself.

Tim, the point I want to make is that the Holy Spirit "is, was, and is to come," in a sense. In the Old Testament he spoke to Abimelech and Pharaoh to make them realize Sarah was Abraham's wife (Genesis 20:3; 12:17). When God called his prophets (Amos, for example), he spoke through them by his Spirit (Amos 3:3; 7:14-16; Jeremiah 1:1-10; Isaiah 6:8; Numbers 11:26-30). When David was selected as king of Israel, the Spirit of God directed Samuel to choose him (1 Samuel 16:1, 13). When a prophet confronts a rebellious king or an unrighteous people, priest, or judge, the Spirit gives him the message and the courage and strength to do it (1 Samuel 12:1; Numbers 11:26-30). When people are downcast and despondent, the Spirit of God lifts them up (Psalms 42:5; 30:1-2, 11-12; Isaiah 40:28-31). In other words, the Holy Spirit was and is God active in the life of the individual and within the Old Testament believing community. God the Holy Spirit is everywhere, and "in him we live and move and have our being" (Psalm 139:7; Acts 17:28).

Now, the "new thing" about the Holy Spirit in the New Testament church and the church of today is this. With the advent of Jesus Christ—his teachings, healings, death/resurrection/ascension—a new age was ushered in. God had now come to live with mankind. In the God/man Jesus Christ he redeemed us—saved us *from* sin *unto* service for him by serving others. The Holy Spirit entered Christ in his fullness at his baptism (Mark 1:10; John 1:32; 3:34). During his ministry our Lord said that God wanted to give us his Holy Spirit (Luke 11:13; 24:49; Acts 1:8; John 14:26; 15:26; 16:7-15). Jesus calls the Holy Spirit the *Paraclete*, the Greek word meaning Helper, Advocate, "the one called alongside to help." He helps us by guiding and instructing us; he empowers believers. But it was not until after the resurrection and ascension that our Lord said that he would "pour out" his Spirit upon his followers (John 7:39; 14:16-17, 25-26; 15:26; 16:7-15; Luke 23:49; Acts 1:8; 2:4). This happened on the Day of Pentecost (Acts 2:1-39). The Holy Spirit, who had already been actively working through Christ, his disciples, and in the world, manifested his presence in a unique way. Read Acts chapter two and see. Unusual visions, revelations, and sounds accompanied the gift of the fullness of the Spirit to the church.

Tim, I was always a bit confused when I was your age because some ministers and Christians talked about being "filled with the Spirit" and "baptized by the Spirit." I visualized a liquid being poured into me or over me. But the Spirit of God is a person, not a liquid. To be filled with the Spirit means to *allow him to take control* by opening all areas of our lives to him (Ephesians 4:18, 30—5:2; 5:17-21). When people were baptized in New Testament times (whether by immersion or with water poured on their heads) this symbolized the washing away of sin and the beginning of a new life in Christ (Romans 6:3-4; Colossians 2:12). In a similar manner, being baptized by the Holy Spirit means allowing the Holy Spirit to transform our lives—by casting out the evil spirit of indifference to God and rebellion against him and leading us in obedience to Christ (Luke 11:24-26; Romans 6:12-19; 8:5-17; Galatians 5:16-25).

So the Holy Spirit was at work in you, Tim, and brought you to confess Christ as Savior and Lord. And when you opened your heart to Christ, the Holy Spirit moved in more fully (John 3:3-5; Matthew 16:15-17; 1 Corinthians 2:11-16; 12:3; Romans 8:14-17). As you permit Christ to take over, your life will be controlled and directed more and more by the Holy Spirit.

Since the Christian life is a dynamic, growing experience, as you learn more about God through his Word, through ordinary living and reading, and through association with other Christians, you will come to understand more about what it means to be obedient to Christ (2 Peter 3:18; Ephesians 4:15-16; Philippians 3:12-16; Acts 17:11; 1 Peter 2:2; 1 Timothy 2:15; 3:14-17). Therefore, Tim, being "filled with the Spirit" must be a daily experience, one that is always growing and changing (Philippians 3:12-14).

In retrospect, your ideas about what you thought constituted a good skier or tennis player are much different today from last year. Likewise, what it means to surrender your life to Christ and to let the Holy Spirit lead you is also different today from what it was a year ago. Sanctification, being set apart from the "world" to serve Christ, is a lifetime growing process (2 Thessalonians 2:13; 1 Peter 1:2; Romans 6:13;

Philippians 2:12-13; 1 Corinthians 15:58). While our decision to surrender to the leadership of the Holy Spirit may occur at a specific point in time, we must allow the Spirit to direct and empower us *daily*—each day calls for a new surrender (Luke 9:23; Psalm 61:8).

Interestingly, in the New Testament the Holy Spirit is closely associated with the revelation of God through Jesus Christ. In John's Gospel, for example, our Lord says that some of the tasks of the Spirit are to teach us the things of Christ, to "guide us into all truth," and to glorify Christ (John 14:25-26; 16:13-15). In Acts, where the apostles' preaching is recorded, you'll find that when they preached the gospel and individuals received Christ, the Holy Spirit was given to them, and often the new believer spoke ecstatically and in an unknown language (Acts 2:1-11; 4:31; 5:32; 8:14-17; 10:44-45, et al.) This "language," however, was understood by others, so the gift of "tongues" (as it is called in the King James Version of the Bible) was given by God in the early church to communicate the faith (Acts 2:1-11). Most biblical scholars agree that this unusual sign was given by God to attest to the historic event of Pentecost with its outpouring of the Spirit into the hearts of believers and the church. When men and women are filled or completely yielded to the Holy Spirit's control, they experience amazing vitality and joy. And Paul adds, God's Spirit gives us power, love, and self-discipline (2 Timothy 1:7; see also Acts 1:8; Romans 5:5; 15:13; Galatians 5:22; Titus 2:6).

In addition to the gift of tongues being associated with Pentecost when the gospel was communicated to Jews from many nations, scholars associate the gift with ecstatic speech uttered by some who received the Holy Spirit (1 Corinthians 12—14; Acts 10:45-46; 19:6). (Those who speak with tongues are said to have the gift of *glossolalia*, the Greek word for speaking in tongues.) While Paul addressed himself to problems this gift created in the church at Corinth, he recognized it as a legitimate gift which was bestowed on some believers (1 Corinthians 12:10). He urged, though, that it can be exercised primarily in private devotions (1 Corinthians 14:2-4, 18-19). When ecstatic speech is expressed in church, Paul insisted that someone be present to interpret (1 Corinthians 14:5, 13). While the majority of Christians in the church do not speak in tongues, for a significant minority in all denominations this experience has been an enriching one. (Those who have this gift call themselves charismatic. The word is from the Greek and means a "gift freely given" by God.) While I am not a charismatic, I do try to be sensitive to the Holy Spirit's leadership and guidance, as I know you are, too, Tim.

We have to resist oversimplifying the experience of being filled with the Spirit. It's not an experience as easy to obtain as snow cones or cotton candy at the county fair. Preconditions precede the infilling—such as searching one's heart, making wrongs right, resisting temptation, choosing the best, and yielding unconditionally to what we understand to be the will of God (Luke 24:49). You will probably meet a few charismatic Christians who will insist that if you are "truly" filled with the Spirit you'll "get the gift of tongues." Most Christians, however, do not equate the fullness of the Spirit with tongues. The New Testament doesn't. So far as we know, our Lord never spoke with tongues and no one would deny that he was filled with the Spirit and completely yielded to the Spirit's control. Interestingly, while Paul acknowledges that he spoke with tongues, he identifies "faith, hope, and love" as the three top virtues. And he says that the greatest gift, the one we should strive to attain, is *love* (1 Corinthians 12:1—13:13; compare 12:4-11 and Romans

116

12:6-8; Ephesians 4:11-16). Paul says that if we love our neighbor, we have fulfilled the whole law (Galatinas 5:14). James calls actively loving one's neighbor fulfilling the "royal law" (James 2:8).

It's easy to overlook the ordinary processes by which God works, through the give-and-take (mostly give) within family, community, and church. Human gifts must be developed; they don't grow overnight like Jonah's gourd! Just as mother has perfected her "gift" of being a gracious hostess (including her tasteful cooking!), so spiritual gifts are developed over a period of time. It is true that there are dramatic conversions like that of the apostle Paul, as well as crisis experiences in which we surrender and submit to God's Spirit. But it takes years to develop the kind of gifts he had, gifts of teaching, preaching, encouragement, and support that we see in his letters (Galatians 1:18; 2:1). As Christians we are all indwelt by the same Spirit (1 Corinthians 12:4, 8-11, 13; Ephesians 4:4). And he gives each of us different gifts, as well as the potential for developing them (Romans 15:13). But unless we work at it, they will remain merely potentials and we will grieve the Holy Spirit (Ephesians 5:30).

Let me point out some things about the relationship between the believer and the Holy Spirit. First, remember that our bodies are the temples of the Holy Spirit—he lives in us (1 Corinthians 3:16; 6:19; 2 Corinthians 1:22, 6:16; 2 Timothy 1:14). Therefore, we should take good care of ourselves—physically, mentally, spiritually, and socially. Tim, you do a much better job of caring for your physical body than I do: you maintain a healthy balance. But there is always the danger of going to extremes in these matters. Some engage in physical activity (recreation or hobby) to excess. Others become overindulgent intellectually, neglecting the spiritual, physical, and social aspects of their lives. Still others define "spiritual" so narrowly that they feel compelled either to be at church, engaged in a church activity, or reading the Bible or some religious book. How unlike Jesus and the great men and women of faith! As a pastor I often found individuals who used religion as a means of escape—wives who neglected their husbands and children to "do God's work"; husbands who neglected or "lost" their wives and children to save others (Ephesians 5:21-33; 1 Timothy 5:8); young people who were "holy," but utterly irresponsible when it came to helping parents with chores about the house (Ephesians 6:1-3). All of life is sacred. It's no accident that Jesus told us loving our neighbor is like loving God. Martin Luther said that our nearest neighbor is our wife, husband, and children. Or to paraphrase James, "Spirituality *without* healthy, helpful relationships and interaction with the family and others is worthless"—it's a contradiction in terms (James 2:26).

If anyone professes to be a "spiritual Christian" (filled with the Spirit) the way to prove it to God and others is "to act justly and love mercy, and to walk humbly with ... God"—by demonstrating it in one's dealing with others (Micah 6:8; Matthew 12:7; James 1:25-27; 2:14-17). That's why I said people outside or inside the church who act as "Monday morning quarterbacks" of the church's program should put their example where their mouth is! Anyone can criticize, but Christian virtues must be integrated into one's life and demonstrated. That is why God gave us his Holy Spirit—to equip us to bear fruit.

Second, God's Spirit confirms within our own spirit that we are truly a child of God (Romans 8:16). Indeed, we are "sealed" by the Holy Spirit. That is, the Spirit's presence in our hearts is a "guarantee"—a first installment of the blessings in store for us, our guarantee of immortality. Someday God in Christ will fully redeem us (Ephesians 4:30; 1:13; 2 Corinthians 1:22; 5:5; Ephesians 1:13-14). There is no reason why a person should be plagued with doubt and uncertainty, since our salvation is based on what God did in Christ, not on anything we do. John says with confidence, "We are God's children now!" (1 John 3:2). This is a personal confidence that we have which unbelievers cannot really understand (1 Corinthians 1:18, 22-24; 2 Corinthians 2:14-16; 4:3-6).

Tim, it might be appropriate to inject here that being a Christian and being Christlike are not synonymous. When we confess Christ as Savior and Lord, we become Christians (Romans 10:8-9). But the process of becoming Christlike is a never-ending task. Even Paul said at the close of his life that "Christ Jesus came into the world to save sinners; of whom I am chief" (1 Timothy 1:15). I'll talk about this in another letter.

Third, the Holy Spirit intercedes for us before the Father (Romans 8:26-27). Just as Jesus assured Peter that he would pray for Peter in his hour of trial, so our Lord, the Great High Priest who sits at God's right hand, intercedes for us (Luke 22:32; Hebrews 1:3; 2:14-18; 4:14-16; 1 John 2:1).

Fourth, the Holy Spirit gives us strength—power to do God's will (Luke 24:49; Romans 15:13, 19; Ephesians 3:7, 20; 2 Timothy 1:7; 2 Peter 1:3). He enables us to walk in the ways of the Lord, bearing the fruit of the Spirit—love, joy, peace, patience, kindness, goodness, faithfulness, gentleness, self-control (Galatians 5:22-23). Commit 2 Timothy 1:7 to memory, Tim. Draw on God's unlimited resources.

Fifth, the Holy Spirit acts as a convincer, convicting us of "sin, righteousness, and judgment" (John 16:8-11). Feelings of anxiety and guilt about wrongs we have done is God at work through our conscience—his Holy Spirit convicting us and urging us to "make things right" (Romans 2:15; 1 Timothy 2:19; 4:1-2).

As I mentioned earlier, the Holy Spirit convinces us that we are sinners who need to repent and accept God's offer of forgiveness in Christ. We're not aware of this at the time, but in retrospect we can see it. An unknown poet expressed this truth beautifully in the hymn we sing:

> I sought the Lord, and afterward I knew
> He moved my soul to seek him, seeking me;
> It was not I that found, O Savior true;
> No, I was found of thee.

Sixth, the indwelling Spirit works in us for our sanctification. (Remember, to sanctify means "to make holy.") God who has chosen us in Christ also wishes to make us holy (1 Peter 1:2; 2 Thessalonians 2:13). Actually, when God looks at us, he sees us as being perfect "in Christ," as already holy (1 Corinthians 1:30). But, practically, God expects us to become more and more holy by obeying the Holy Spirit who uses the Word of God to accomplish this (John 17:17; Ephesians 6:17). We are called to yield not only our mind and will, but also our total physical body to righteous living (Romans 12:1-2).

Tim, sanctification is both a crisis and a process. We may experience a "great leap forward" by making a crucial decision for Christ, one that changes our behavior and/or our life's direction. But *most* growth is gradual; our daily walk in obedience to Christ confirms and consolidates our crucial commitments. As we read the Word of God regularly, the Holy Spirit shows us what behavior patterns need to be developed, modified, or forsaken. He works through the Word, which is sharper than a finely honed sword, to help us mature and grow in Christ (Ephesians 6:17; 2 Timothy 2:15; Hebrews 4:12-13; 1 Peter 2:2).

One thing more about sanctification. Occasionally you'll hear people talk about the need to surrender utterly to Christ and receive the fullness of the Holy Spirit. This may give the impression that "surrendering" is something you do once and for all. In a way I agree, but in another way this idea is misleading. I like to compare sanctification to marriage. I committed myself to your mother on our wedding day, but our relationship has been a growing one—in "spurts" and gradually. A successful marriage requires not only an *initial* commitment, but also daily renewal and much hard work. Likewise, the Christian makes *one* commitment to Christ, at which time the Holy Spirit comes to live within. But he takes increasing control as we yield to him and follow his leadership.

What have I said, then, Tim? The Holy Spirit is a person, the third person of the Trinity. He has always been active in the world—in the lives of individuals, working within them to accomplish God's will. The Holy Spirit dwelt in Christ in all of his fullness. After our Lord ascended into heaven, he and the Father sent forth the Holy Spirit to indwell believers. In fact, it is by the unique workings of God's Spirit that we come to a saving knowledge of God in Christ. He enables us to see the truth and to confess that "Jesus is Lord!"

Being filled with the Holy Spirit means allowing him to *control* and *direct* our lives. Disciplined discipleship is to be our daily experience.

Some of the truths associated with the person and work of the Holy Spirit are: (1) We are the temple of the Spirit and the proof of his indwelling is the good fruit we bear. (2) The Spirit confirms with our own spirit that we are indeed God's children now, and his presence is a guarantee that we will share the glories of heaven with Christ. (3) The Spirit intercedes for us before the Father. (4) The Spirit gives us power and strength to live and witness for Christ. (5) The Spirit convicts us when we sin and leads us back into fellowship with God and his people. (6) The Spirit is at work in us, sanctifying us, making us holy—more like Christ.

Finally, Tim, I refer you to a couple of good passages in Paul's letters—Ephesians 4:1—5:21 and Galatians 5:13—6:10. There Paul urges us to be filled with the Spirit and to allow him to lead us. In this way we will bear fruit that glorifies God and Christ, as well as know the joy that comes from walking in obedience to him.

Peace, Tim.

I love you,
Dad

Becoming a Christian

Dear Tim,

It occurred to me that I should write something to you about "becoming" and "being" a Christian, even though you have been a Christian for several years. Becoming a Christian is the most important decision anyone can make. It's more important than choosing a wife or a career, because these choices are both affected by your commitment to Christ. Accepting Christ as Savior automatically includes accepting him as the Lord of your life. In a real sense this means that you're no longer your own *boss*—for you must now submit to the lordship of Jesus Christ (1 Corinthians 6:19-20; 7:22-23).

But allowing him to rule is not a burdensome thing. Really, everyone is ruled or dominated by someone or something—some set of values, some philosophy of life or belief system. Those who do not accept the lordship of Christ end up with a "lord"—but of a lesser sort.

Jesus issued an open-ended invitation:

Come to me, all of you who are tired from carrying heavy loads, and I will give you rest. Take my yoke and put it on you, and learn from me, because I am gentle and humble in spirit; and you will find rest. For the yoke I will give you is easy, and the load I will put on you is light (Matthew 11:28-30, TEV)

It's not a matter of whether we'll "bear a yoke" or not—all do. The question is *which* and *whose* yoke will we bear? The choice is ours. However, only the yoke of Christ can be borne with comparative ease because it brings us internal peace and harmony. Furthermore, obedience to him frees us from bondage to surrogate "gods" that oppress and destroy us (Psalm 106:36; Ezekiel 14:4-5; Jeremiah 2:11, 13). Surrogate gods are substitute gods (idols) that compete for our allegiance.

The poet, George Matheson wrote:

> Make me a captive Lord, and then I shall be free;
> Force me to render up my sword, and I shall conqueror be.
> I sink in life's alarms when by myself I stand;
> Imprison me within thine arms, and strong shall be my hand.

Tim, it's only as we surrender to the lordship of Christ that we truly find freedom (John 8:31-32). Freedom is not something that can be found in isolation. It can only be experienced through proper relationships—and it begins with God. You've tinkered around with machinery enough to know that if gears don't mesh, you've got a problem. Remember when you were learning how to drive and you shifted gears without properly engaging the clutch? Just the thought of gears grinding makes me cringe! But when the gears are properly engaged—how sweet it is! The car runs beautifully. Likewise, when we are reconciled to God—rightly related to him—how beautiful life is. That is real freedom.

Becoming a Christian begins by accepting God's offer of

forgiveness and reconciliation in Christ. Reconciliation, however, must be both a *vertical* and a *horizontal* experience—being rightly related *both* to God and man (James 2:14-16; 1 John 4:20-21). Fortunately, we are not left to grope on our own as to what a right relationship involves. God has given us his Word, the Bible; and we have a lifetime to study it and learn about him and his will and purposes for each of us, as well as for his church. In relationships with others—through fellowship, Bible study, prayer, worship, sharing in the sacraments, and service—we grow into mature, responsible Christians (Hebrews 10:25; Acts 2:42; 2 Timothy 3:15-16; 1 Thessalonians 4:9-12).

Becoming a Christian does not mean that one becomes a "perfect" individual by any means. We must confess what surely is painfully obvious to us as well as to others—that while we profess to be Christians, we are *still* sinners. Because you and I realize this, we don't expect perfection of each other, nor do we expect it of others. But we know, also, that God is at work in all of us to draw us closer to Christ (Philippians 1:6; 2:12-13; John 15:1-2). We work together with God in the world, praying for and supporting one another (1 Corinthians 3:9; 2 Corinthians 13:7-9; Colossians 1:9; 1 Thessalonians 5:17; James 5:17; Matthew 25:31-46).

Tim, as you're well aware, each of us is uniquely different. Each comes to Christ from a different background—intellectually, socially, economically, and culturally. But no matter what our background, we must all come to Christ in simple faith and trust (Mark 10:15; Ephesians 2:8-9; 3:17). Amazingly, the infinite Christ meets each individual's unique needs. Of course we all share the basic need for forgiveness. Only the proud and self-righteous refuse to come to him; they are difficult to move (Mark 2:17; Luke 18:9-14; John 9:39-41). They see no need for forgiveness. They're too busy finding fault, criticizing, and condemning others, conveniently oblivious to their own faults. I remember a former student at Maryville College who argued with me after class one day. (I taught biblical literature at Maryville.) He insisted that I convince him of his need for Christ. He believed that he was already *better than* many Christians he knew. After a long fruitless discussion I finally said, "Go away! Come back and see me when you realize that *you* are a sinner; then you'll be glad to learn about God's gracious offer of forgiveness in Christ."

Sometimes people boldly proclaim that they are atheists or agnostics, defying God and finding fault with him. I often wonder what went wrong in their lives. Who let them down? Was it their mother or father? A trusted friend? Have they themselves "messed up," and are they unwilling to face up to it? Just as guilt often makes individuals avoid people to whom they owe money, or whom they have wronged, so people who are unwilling to humble themselves and repent avoid God and the church. The only alternatives to faith in God are avoidance, denial, and/or attack. Subconsciously or consciously they believe that so long as they do not acknowledge God, they can live as they please. They feel they don't have to worry about "doing justly, loving mercy," not to mention "walking humbly with God" (Micah 6:8). Like the male character in the TV serial *Soap* who snapped his fingers and declared himself *not there*, some feel they can snap God out of existence. But it just can't be done. We either face God now as redeemer, or we meet him later as judge (Hebrews 9:27; 1 Peter 4:5; Acts 10:42; 17:31; Romans 2:5; 14:10-12; 2 Corinthians 5:10; Jude 15).

So then, Tim, we come to Christ because through him God offers us forgiveness, and because we want the fullness of life that comes through reconciliation (Luke 24:46-47; 2

Corinthians 5:17-21; Colossians 1:14). But, in addition, we're motivated by a sense of gratitude (Psalm 116:12-13). Only a psychopath or sociopath—one who does not know right from wrong—would deny his need for forgiveness. Thus far I've met only a couple of people like that. I met one when I was a member of the youth group in a Presbyterian Church in Philadelphia. We used to conduct open-air evangelistic meetings at Rayburn Plaza, not far from city hall. This was shortly after the Second World War. Following one meeting I talked to a man from skid row who came back to our church. He looked me square in the eye and said, "I've never sinned; I have nothing to repent of." The other person was a student who wrote in her socio-autobiography, "I've never done anything I'm really sorry about!" As I mentioned earlier, if one has never sinned he doesn't need a Savior. But as the apostle John says, "If we say that we have not sinned, we make a liar out of God, and his word is not in us" (1 John 1:10, TEV).

God's Word states that each of us is a sinner and that this results in estrangement or separation from God (Romans 1:21-32; 1 Corinthians 1:21; Ephesians 4:18). Because of this, God sent his Son to die in our place, to bear our sins in his own body on the cross (1 Peter 2:21-25; 2 Corinthians 5:21). Then, on the third day, he raised Christ from the dead (Romans 1:4; Hebrews 13:20; 1 Corinthians 15:3-4). It is the height of ingratitude, therefore, to reject God's offer of forgiveness in Christ.

Jesus told a parable about a man who gave a great banquet (Luke 14:15-24). He invited many guests, but they made excuses and did not come. So the host invited those from the "highways and hedges"—common people from the streets—to come in and join in the feasting. In the parable, Jesus was holding a mirror before the "Pharisees and

Scribes" of his day—the self-righteous who would not enter the kingdom. He was telling them that God would make up his kingdom without them. And today those who refuse to accept God's offer of forgiveness and who refuse to say "thank you" to him also exclude themselves from the kingdom.

The writer of Hebrews says that it is not only a grave insult to God to reject his offer of salvation, but it is a foolish thing, because one does it to his own peril (Hebrews 2:3). Becoming a Christian, Tim, is not only the wisest step you've taken, because it means a full abundant life for you, but it is the most meaningful way to say "thank you" to God for all he has done and will do for you in Christ.

Tim, I should say something about the different ways individuals come to know Christ. Since individuals and groups are different from one another, it is only natural that individuals will come to Christ in a variety of ways. You, Steve, Susie, and Debbi came to know Christ through your home-life, the church, and through individuals you've met. Each of you participated in something like a "communicants class." Eventually all of you made a profession of faith in your teen years. You may not have been fully aware of all the ramifications of your decision, but in essence you received Christ into your hearts and said "thank you" to God. Later each of you has had experiences with Christ which have deepened that commitment, and I trust that experiences like these will continue. In some cases, a conscious commitment to Christ does not come until later. This was my experience. I went to Sunday school and church, and I was even baptized in a Baptist church when I was fourteen. But I really didn't make a conscious commitment to Christ until I was eighteen years old. Howard, Debbi's husband made a profession of faith and was baptized when he was twenty-four, whereas, Jack, Susan's husband, professed his faith as a young teenager.

Whether one is raised in a Christian family or not, whether one went through a communicants' class or not, is *not* the crucial thing. All of these things certainly help and I hope you provide these for your children. Knowing *about* God and Christ is not the same as *knowing* him. Emile Brunner, a famous theologian, said that one might know the theology of Paul and even teach it, and still not be a committed Christian. One of my seminary professors said that he didn't accept Christ as his Savior and Lord until he was out in his first parish! Priests, ministers, elders, and deacons have also had similar experiences. The crucial experience is having a living, meaningful, personal experience with Christ.

Tim, not only do people come to Christ in different ways, but they use different expressions when they talk about their Christian experience. Thanks to President Carter, the expression "being born again" has become more widely known today. Jesus talked to Nicodemus about his need to be "born again" (John 3:1-16). Interestingly, Nicodemus, an elder within the Jewish synagogue, was familiar with this expression. Jews went about telling Gentiles that they needed to be "born again." They also insisted that Gentiles needed to be "washed" (baptized), cleansed of their sinful ways. But when Jesus told Nicodemus that he needed to be "born again," he was shocked. This confirms what I said earlier; one can be an elder or officer in a church and still be outside of the kingdom. At any rate, the point I want to make is that the concept of the "new birth" is a legitimate metaphor. It explains what happens to us when the Holy Spirit leads us to make a profession of faith in Christ. The new birth marks the beginning of a new relationship with God through Christ.

Sometimes there is a long "gestation period" before a conscious profession of faith is made—before one is "born again." The Spirit of God, who works within us to bring us to Christ, may receive a quick affirmative response from us or he may have to struggle with us for a long time. We may or may not have been nurtured in the faith within the family, the church, and through fellowship with Christian friends. As the apostle Paul said, someone plants the seed (gospel), another waters, others cultivate the soil, but ultimately it is God who brings the "new life" into being (1 Corinthians 3:5-9). Look at the parable of the sower, or as some call it, the parable of the soils (Mark 4:2-20). There Jesus says that once we respond to him in faith, once the new life begins, the responsibility for how the new life takes shape rests primarily on our shoulders (although I believe it is the responsibility of the Christian community, the church, to nurture the individual in the faith). The church is like a mother to the "newborn" child in Christ. Nonetheless, we determine by the decisions we make along the way, by the way we react to the trials, temptations, and challenges of life, whether we will bear fruit or not.

Another important thing to keep in mind regarding the "new birth" is that it is only the beginning of life, as I mentioned above. As a newborn infant, you would have died if you had not been fed and nurtured by your mother and the family. Similarly, your Christian life will be stunted and even die unless it is fed and nurtured through prayer, fellowship in the church, and the reading of God's Word, and exercised in living your faith and engaging in Christian service (Acts 2:42; 1 Peter 2:2; Mark 8:34-36; John 12:24-26).

But, Tim, other concepts besides that of the new birth are also used in the New Testament. Paul often speaks about individuals who were "converted" to Christ as a result of his preaching (Romans 16:5; 1 Corinthians 16:5). To be converted means to be "turned around"—turned from going away *from* God *to* walking in his direction. The prodigal son, Zacchaeus, and Paul are all classic examples of individuals who were "converted." In reality, we must all do an about face—from living for oneself to living for Christ. Being converted is another way of describing what happens to us when we decide to become Christians.

Still another expression is being "saved." The Philippian jailer asked Paul and Silas, "Men, what must I do to be saved?" (Acts 16:30, RSV). Once again, it is Christ who saves us by his sacrificial death (Acts 4:12; Ephesians 2:8-9). When we accept God's offer of salvation in Christ, we are saved *from* a life of bondage to sin and selfishness *to* a life of freedom, joy, and service (Romans 5:10; 10:9-10; John 8:32; Galatians 5:1; 1 Timothy 1:15).

Words such as "reconciled," "justified," and "redeemed" are also used to describe the state of those who put their faith and trust in Christ (2 Corinthians 5:20; Ephesians 2:16; Galatians 2:16; 3:13; Romans 3:24; 5:1). As you can see, Tim, various figures of speech can be used to describe the experience of becoming a Christian. Each expression helps us understand the Christian's initial experience. Each one has profound meaning, as well as validity. For the most part, the terms that are used depend on the knowledge and perspective of the individual and the denomination that is instrumental in helping the person come to Christ.

Summing up, Tim, *becoming* a Christian is the most important decision you have made because it affects all others. Everyone has a master and bears a yoke, but Christ is the best master because his yoke is the most worthwhile and the easiest to bear. He gives us true freedom. *Becoming* a Christian begins with the vertical relationship and it is lived out on a horizontal plane as we interact with others.

As Christians we're far from perfect, Tim. We're merely sinners saved by God's grace. While others may reject God's offer of forgiveness, we acknowledge our sinfulness and need for divine and human forgiveness. We experience forgiveness and newness of life by accepting God's offer of salvation in Christ. People find Christ in different ways, depending on their individual makeup and the group or church that introduces them to Christ. Whether an individual grows into the faith, or whether he has a crisis experience, depends on his social situation and the way God chooses to work in his life. The important thing, Tim, is not *how* it happens, but that it *does* happen—that the individual comes to know Christ as Savior and Lord. The terminology describing the Christian's experience may vary (born again, converted, saved, or whatever) but the important thing is that we *become* a Christian.

In my next letter I'll share some thoughts about *being* a Christian. Until then, take care, Tim.

All my love,
Dad

Letter **13**

Being a Christian

Dear Tim,

In this letter I want to share some thoughts about *being* a Christian.

As an infant and child you were nurtured mostly by mother. Your older brother and sisters and I played an important part in your development, too—for good or for ill. The last time we saw Steve, we were doing some reminiscing about the trials and tribulations of "growing up." He talked about the difficulties he and Debbi used to have with you when they "child sat." You frustrated Steve because you wouldn't listen to him. When he tried to get you to do something, such as clean your plate at mealtime, you just *refused* to do it—like any red-blooded American child!

Debbi also tried her hand at disciplining you, although her tactics were different. "Timmy, clean your plate! I'll give you five minutes, and if you're not finished, off to your bedroom!" But alas, her hard line was no more successful than Steve's. Oddly enough, I was never that strict with either of them. Do you think, in retrospect, that firmness with you was their way of telling me, "Dad, you were too lax in disciplining us"? I guess mom would say so.

But your nurture—physical, intellectual, social, and spiritual—didn't stop when you reached adolescence, when you could pretty much fend for yourself. Quite the contrary; your growth since then has been phenomenal—and I might say that I'm quite pleased. Keep growing in the same directions! As long as you live you'll continue to grow and develop greater competencies in your chosen vocation, as well as in a variety of areas as opportunities to work, study, and travel open up to you—as you interact with old and newly made friends.

Just as your vocational and social life will enable you to grow in those spheres, active participation in the Christian community will enable you to grow spiritually. Actually, your spiritual growth should occur simultaneously with the growth in other areas of your life, since Christianity ought to be integrated into all of life. Growth in Christ is a lifetime process—a continuous adventure with God.

I'm reminded of the summer after Steve went through confirmation classes at the Presbyterian church in Sterling, Kansas. I asked him, "Steve, would you like to go to summer church camp?"

"What would I do there, dad?" he asked.

"Well, Steve," I said, "you'd get to make a lot of new friends, participate in sports, and have a chance to learn more about your faith through Bible study and the like."

"Gee, dad," he said, "I learned all that stuff in confirmation class!"

Unfortunately, many people feel that way after they have made a profession of faith in Christ and joined the church. (What if Einstein or Bach had said that they had learned all they needed to know about science or music after their first course or beginning lessons?) Of course you know better than that, and so does Steve.

134

Unfortunately, Tim, you'll meet individuals who were exposed to a strict interpretation of Christianity, either in their home or church. Aside from that childhood exposure, they never received an accurate understanding of the faith—nor did they take the opportunity to obtain one as they grew older. Quite often they are rather caustic in their criticism of Christianity, but the content of their criticism betrays their abysmal ignorance of it. They are guilty of premature closure. These same individuals would never think of being content with an elementary or inadequate understanding in other areas of knowledge.

When we lived in Tennessee I visited a chemical engineer, in his fifties, who was alienated from God and the church largely because his knowledge of Christianity was immature and erroneous. His childhood exposure to the faith came through attending a church where an uneducated "hell-fire and damnation" minister preached. It was too bad he had not taken the trouble to gain an adult understanding of Christianity before he decided to reject it.

Being a Christian means continuous growth, being forever open to God and Christ (Ephesians 4:15; 2 Peter 3:18). It also means allowing Christian insights (attitudes and values) to affect our decision-making and behavior. While God calls us to pattern our lives after Christ's, we have to realize that we will invariably fall short of our goal (Romans 7:15-25). Because of our finitude (limited knowledge) and our human frailty, we will sin against our fellowman, and therefore, God. Therefore, we must continually ask for forgiveness, seek to make restitution when possible, and get on with our Christian walk (1 John 1:9—2:6).

My good friends, Ira and Hugh, are often annoyed by what they feel is a preoccupation with sin on the part of ministers. They object to the prayers of confession pastors formulate that are often so specific and that compel all the worshipers to confess sins, whether they are guilty or not. The worshiper is made to feel worthless. My friend John feels the same way about his minister, although in his case it is not the prayers but the sermons. His minister dwells on the imagined sins and shortcomings of his parishioners so much that they leave church feeling rejected by God.

I know what they mean. I was leading the morning worship service at a church in Williamsport one Sunday. After we had recited the prayer of confession which the host pastor had prepared, I asked the congregation, "My goodness, are we *that* bad?"

While we should not indict all for the particular sins and shortcomings of some, nonetheless we do need to remind ourselves that even though we are professing Christians, we are still sinners. This will keep us from getting too puffed up, too self-righteous, and it will help us to persevere in our quest for genuine holiness. Something our Lord said should help keep us humble. He was speaking about a servant's duty. He said, "When you have done all you have been told to do, say, 'We are ordinary servants; we have only done our duty' " (Luke 17:7-10, TEV); see also 1 Corinthians 4:7 and Romans 12:3). And, as Christians, we are expected to be servants.

Furthermore, I would add that we need to inform non-Christians every chance we get that "saints" are sinners, too! (The word "saint" in Greek means "holy one," one set apart *from* serving self *to* serving God and others.)

Too often non-Christians, as well as uninformed Christians, point to something a Christian has done or said, saying, "And he calls himself a Christian!" The assumption is that a Christian is one who is perfect. Impossible! Humans can never achieve perfection. If we could, God would not have sent Christ to redeem us (Romans 7:21-25; 8:1-11). We are Christians because we have accepted God's offer of forgiveness in Christ, not because we ourselves are perfect (2 Corinthians 5:16-21; Ephesians 2:8-9). As soon as we make sinlessness or perfection the primary criteria for acceptance with God, we automatically exclude ourselves and everyone else from the kingdom. Furthermore, we are guilty of saying that the grace and mercy of God are no longer necessary. In reality, this amounts to saying we are "saved by works."

No, Christians are not, and never will be perfect in this life. But because we're not perfect doesn't mean we are not Christians. When we do not follow God's will for our lives, when we break his laws and fail to live by Christian principles, we are not being Christlike. But this does not mean that we have ceased being Christian. Failing to be Christlike is not something of which we should be proud, but unfortunately it is something all Christians experience. Nonetheless, as I said earlier, we must continually strive to be Christlike, to be holy—not holier than thou (1 Corinthians 6:11; John 17:7; 1 Thessalonians 5:23; Matthew 5:43-48; Hebrews 12:5; Philippians 3:12-14).

Being a Christian involves continually yielding ourselves, our minds, and our wills to Christ. Paul says it involves presenting our bodies to Christ as "living sacrifices," and being "transformed by the renewing of your mind" (Romans 12:1-2; Ephesians 4:22-24). Another analogy he uses is that of changing clothes. We are told to put off the old self and to put on the new self (Ephesians 4:22-24; Colossians 3:5-11; Hebrews 12:1-2). This is not something that can be accomplished overnight. It is a process that requires daily renewal (Matthew 6:28-34).

Tim, do you remember those "Indian burial mounds" we

had behind our house near your skateboard ramp? Those piles of stones and rocks we accumulated when we prepared the front and back lawns of our house and sowed grass seed? Well after seven years, I finally decided the only way I was going to get rid of them was to move them one shovel at a time. Now I've got them all in one place and, hopefully, I'll mix them with cement to form the floor of that outbuilding mother has been wanting me to build. Renewing our minds and bringing our lives into conformity to the will of God is accomplished in the same way—one day at a time (Philippians 3:12-16).

Occasionally, Tim, you'll come across some Christians, ministers and laymen, who insist that after you've become a Christian, you must have another unique experience with God, one in which you surrender *completely* to Christ—body, mind, heart, and will. This experience of total commitment or surrender is often referred to as a "second work of grace."

In part, I would say "right on." Many people do have a second crisis experience. But as Claude Ries, my Greek New Testament professor at Houghton College insisted, this second crisis experience must be followed by a *process*—that of *daily* renewal, or surrender. While many do indeed have a "second" experience with Christ that proves to be pivotal and crucial in their Christian experience, I believe the Bible and the overwhelming experience of most Christians supports the view that we undergo *a series* of "surrendering experiences." As I mentioned earlier when writing about sanctification, growth comes through insights and experiences with Christ and others. Some of these constitute "great leaps forward," but all must be followed with periods of "routine growth."

Tim, perhaps I could use an analogy from your own

experience. Do you remember when you decided to stop eating junk food? Was it a one-time experience? Yes and No. Yes, the decision was made on a specific day. No, it has been something that you have had to renew daily. And I might add, what you consider "junk food" has probably changed, permitting you to eat some more foods now than you did in the past, but also requiring that you drop others. Therefore, just as each day is a new experience, so is our commitment to Christ something that must be renewed each day.

To put it still another way, think of your skiing. When you make new strides in the sport, it's not accomplished by a singular second decision—one that does not require the acquisition of further techniques and skills. Your decision to be a professional skier has demanded that you recommit yourself daily to a rigorous training schedule. Unfortunately, Tim, there is no easy road to anything—including Christian maturity! Don't fall for any "line" propagated by anyone offering you instant success or victory without effort. Jesus said, "For the gate is narrow and the way is hard, that leads to life"—and you can trust his Word (Matthew 7:14, RSV; see also Luke 9:23; 1 Corinthians 9:24-27; 15:30-31; 2 Corinthians 4:7-18).

As you read the Gospels and the other New Testament writings you'll find that being a Christian involves internalizing certain virtues. These virtues, as well as the vices God wants us to avoid, are mentioned repeatedly. Why? Because the churches to which the apostles wrote were composed of "saints" who were prone to forget and stray—prone to yield to the temptations of the flesh and the vanity of the mind (1 John 2:15-17; Romans 12:1-2; Philippians 2:1-11). Christians living in the first century had to be reminded, as we do, of God's commands and expectations. Let me call your attention to one passage in which Paul sums up the virtues to be pursued and the vices to be avoided.

> Now the works of the flesh are plain: fornication, impurity, licentiousness, idolatry, sorcery, enmity, strife, jealousy, anger, selfishness, dissension, party spirit, envy, drunkenness, carousing, and the like. I warn you, as I warned you before, that those who do such things shall not inherit the kingdom of God. But the fruit of the Spirit is love, joy, peace, patience, kindness, goodness, faithfulness, gentleness, self-control; against such there is no law. And those who belong to Christ Jesus have crucified the flesh with its passions and desires (Galatians 5:19-24, RSV).

I could cite scores of passages that say substantially the same thing. The point is, being a Christian calls for constant vigilance and discipline (1 Peter 5:8-11; 2 Peter 1:10; 3:14-18; Philippians 2:12-13; 2 Timothy 1:7; 2:3-5; 1 Corinthians 9:24-27). One never arrives (Philippians 3:12-14). In fact, the apostle Paul found that the longer he lived and the closer he walked with God, the more he became aware of his shortcomings (1 Timothy 1:12-17). But thank God, the more we do so, the more we become aware of God's grace. (Romans 11:33-36; 1 Corinthians 2:9-10; 2 Corinthians 12:1-10).

Tim, in addition to those who promise you easy victory, you will encounter those who would lead you to believe that total commitment to Christ means going into "full-time Christian service." By this they mean you must be a minister or missionary. (These people remind me of some in the early church who taught that *first class* Christians remained virgins and were "married to Christ" and served him in a church vocation. But *second class* Christians were those who married because they could not control the passions of the flesh!) People who talk like that do a lot of harm. They place needless guilt on many young Christians. Let me tell you why I say this.

While I agree that a Christian who gives his full time to a church vocation has a unique calling and that he carries a heavy responsibility within the church, everyone cannot occupy such a position. To use Paul's analogy of the body (the church), "if all were clergymen, to whom would they preach and minister?" Originally Jesus called only twelve apostles, although others were later added to them (Matthew 10:1ff; Acts 1:15-26; Romans 1:1; 16:7, *et al.*). While all who follow Christ do so because God called them by his Spirit into his service, all are not called to be apostles. (The Latin verb "to call" is *vocāre*, from which we get our word "vocation.") From among those whom God has called, some are called to be apostles, prophets, evangelists, pastors, and teachers "to prepare all God's people for the work of Christian service, in order to build up the body of Christ" (Ephesians 4:11-12, TEV). In Romans Paul mentions other gifts such as serving, encouraging, giving (material assistance), leadership, and showing mercy (Romans 12:6-8). And in First Corinthians he mentions additional gifts, notably the ability to speak with wisdom, with knowledge, as well as faith, healing, miraculous powers, discernment, administration, and the ability to speak different languages or tongues (12:4-11; 27-31; 13:1ff.).

While God has given a variety of gifts to the church, and while the apostle Paul lists them in the order of their importance, each gift is essential to the functioning of the body of Christ (1 Corinthians 12:12-30; Ephesians 3:1-13). It is significant to note also, Tim, that these gifts are not confined to so-called "professional clergy"; all are not preachers, teachers, pastors, or evangelists. The important thing is not whether one is a professional clergyman or not, but whether one is faithful in using his gifts and in the position to which God has called him (1 Corinthians 4:2; John 15:1-17).

Actually, Tim, it is misleading to equate total commitment to Christ with church professionals because in God's sight each one of us is called to be a witness by word and deed—this is our primary vocation. How we earn our living is secondary. What is important is that in our secular position we do all to the glory of God—for the well-being of all in society (1 Corinthians 10:31; Colossians 3:17, 23; Ephesians 4:1-16).

When you perform your role as skier with all you've got, relating honestly and helpfully with others, you are witnessing for Christ. But in addition to our witness by a job well done, God expects us to share the gospel. As the apostle Peter said, we should always be ready "to explain the hope" we have in Christ (1 Peter 3:15, TEV). You did this beautifully, for example, when you were a counselor at camp and you shared Christ with the boy in your cabin. You didn't refer him to a professional clergyman; you straightforwardly shared the good news of the gospel.

Finally, being a Christian means taking your place in the church, the body of Christ, and assuming your responsibility there. In a sense, the church is only as strong as its weakest member. That is, unless we know Christ personally, unless we live out in our daily lives our Lord's teachings, and unless each of us assumes a servant role, the church cannot be the kind of servant our Lord wants it to be.

So long as its members believe that "witnessing" is the responsibility only of the minister, the church will be an ineffective instrument in the world. The reason why some churches grow more rapidly than others is that the laymen in them have had a personal experience with Christ and they are actively witnessing by word and deed. They take their Christian calling (vocation) seriously. I'll write something about the church in my next letter.

This has been a rather lengthy letter, but I felt that I had to share these things with you.

Tim, *being* a Christian implies a way of life—continuous growth in Christ. We must allow the Holy Spirit to apply the truths of God's Word to all aspects of our lives, sanctifying, claiming, and using them for God's glory. *Being* a Christian means that we consider others better than ourselves; that we do not become puffed up with pride. After all, Tim, the talents or abilities we have were all gifts given to us by God. But we do have the privilege and responsibility of developing and using them. *Being* a Christian demands constant renewal of our minds—the offering of our entire lives to his service. *Being* totally committed to Christ doesn't mean that we must enter a church vocation, although it may mean this for some. But it does mean that we be totally committed to serving Christ in whatever position he calls us. *Being* a Christian also means that we affiliate with a church and participate actively in its program.

I'll close for now, Tim. God be with you. May you always be true to your calling. May you always be in the process of becoming more like our Lord.

I love you, Tim,
Dad

The Mission of
the Church

Dear Tim,

In this letter I want to share some thoughts about the church. I'm not referring to a specific denomination, but to the church in general, the body of Christ (Romans 10:5; 1 Corinthians 12:27; Ephesians 1:22-23; Colossians 1:18, 24). When we recite the Apostle's Creed we say, "I believe in the holy *catholic* church," which means the *universal* church composed of believers in churches of all denominations. When the Holy Spirit succeeds in bringing us to the place where we affirm "Jesus is Lord," then we become a part of the body of Christ (1 Corinthians 12:3; Romans 10:9-10). As Paul said, "So we, though many, are one body in Christ, and individually members one of another" (Romans 12:5, RSV; see 1 Corinthians 10:16-17; 12:27; Ephesians 4:25). "For by one Spirit we were all baptized into one body . . . . Now you are the body of Christ and individually members of it" (1 Corinthians 12:13, 27, RSV).

Paul used the analogy of the human physical body to illustrate the essential unity we have in Christ, who is the head of the body, the church (1 Corinthians 12:12-26; Ephesians 1:22-23; 4:15-16; 5:23; Colossians 1:18). Just as our bodies are composed of many parts, and each part is essential to the healthy functioning of the body, so each of us is an essential part of the body of Christ, the church.

Elsewhere in Scripture, the apostle Peter likens Christians to building blocks of God's spiritual house or temple, with Christ himself as the chief cornerstone (1 Peter 2:4-10; Mark 12:10). Paul says Christ is the foundation stone upon which the Christian and the church builds (1 Corinthians 3:11). God has given each of us a special gift/talent/or position, as I mentioned in my last letter, and each one makes a positive contribution to his body (1 Corinthians 12:27-30; Romans 12:5-8; Ephesians 4:11-16).

We have been members of various churches. Each of them has included a good mix of people—different age-groups, ethnic backgrounds, socioeconomic classes, and vocations. Each person had unique gifts, strengths, and weaknesses, but together we complemented each other to make up a warm Christian family or community.

As you well know, Tim, the secret to getting something out of any organization is active participation. Our Lord taught in the parable of the talents, or three servants, that one must get involved. We must invest ourselves in kingdom work if we hope to have a meaningful Christian life (Matthew 25:14-30; Luke 19:11-27). As one Christian said to a banker who was a nominal Christian and was complaining that he didn't derive much benefit from his church: "You're a banker; you know what to do. Put more money into your account and you'll get more interest out!" Generally speaking this is true, isn't it, Tim?

Our Lord plainly said, "Your heart [interest] will always be where your riches are" (Matthew 6:21, TEV). You see this principle at work in our own family regarding their jobs. Your brother Steve is dedicated to his art, and his wife,

Nadine, is busy with her school psychology. Your sister Debbi is pursuing her career in interior design, while her husband, Howard, is involved in his successful business. And your sister Susan enjoys her day care position, while her husband, Jack, is seriously involved in school administration. Likewise, unless one gives time, energy, and money to the Lord's work in the church, a person will not derive much benefit from it.

The Lord drove this point home when he said, "If anyone wants to come with me . . . he must forget himself, carry his cross, and follow me" (Mark 8:34, TEV; see Luke 14:27; John 12:24-26). I think we've seen enough of the tragic consequences of those who live by a self-centered, hedonistic philosophy—"do your own thing." The result of living like that is neglect of one's responsibility to others, both within and outside of the family, as well as ultimate self-destruction. Too often, even in the church, some people become more obsessed with their rights than with their responsibilities. We forget God's directive that "nobody should seek his own good, but the good of others" (1 Corinthians 10:24). Whenever we use our gifts or talents for the common good, for those within the body of Christ as well as those without, then we derive a tremendous blessing (Matthew 5:3-12; Mark 8:35). Because we are social beings created for fellowship with God and one another, and to work for the common good, active participation in the church is a must, not an option (1 Corinthians 10:24; John 12:24-26; Hebrews 10:25).

The fourth commandment says, "Remember the sabbath day, to keep it holy" (Exodus 20:8, RSV). Our Lord Jesus went to the synagogue faithfully each Sabbath (Luke 4:16). Of course, Tim, you know the Christian "Sabbath" is our Sunday, or the first day of the week—the Lord's Day (Mark 16:2; Acts 20:7; 1 Corinthians 16:2; Revelation 1:10). It is the day he rose from the dead, bringing life and immortality to light (2 Timothy 1:10). In the early church Christians often gathered daily, as well as on the first day of the week, for instruction, fellowship, holy communion, and prayers (Acts 2:42). It was also customary for one church to help another by taking a collection to relieve the needs of Christians in distress (1 Corinthians 16:2-4). Each one of these elements is essential to a healthy Christian life and a healthy church.

Tim, I am pleased to see that you identify quickly with a church when you locate in a new community. While I have been Presbyterian, mother comes from an Anabaptist background. Many of her kinfolk are in the Brethren Church. Which group you affiliate with is not my chief concern. The important thing is that you do select a church in which you feel you can worship, fellowship, and serve; although my hope is that you'll remain active in a particular denomination so that you can put down roots and maintain continuity. I hope you won't be a "church tramp"; there is little to be gained by flitting from one church to another in a given community. And there is little to be gained by changing from one denomination to another. There is no one perfect church or denomination. They are all made up of human beings! So choose wisely, as I'm sure you will, and serve the Lord with all you've got.

Tim, you've probably already encountered individuals who insist that they "don't have to go to church to be a Christian." Of course only God knows who is and who isn't a Christian. But it is difficult for me to understand how anyone who has even a passing knowledge of the Christian gospel could say that. Paul's analogy of the church as the body of Christ suggests that one cannot sever himself from the body and live.

When I think of the rationalizations some use to evade their responsibility for participating in the Christian church, all sorts of responses come to mind. I wonder whether the individual really understands the gospel, and whether he has accepted God's forgiveness in Christ. This forgiveness was not obtained cheaply; it cost him his life (John 3:16; Colossians 1:22; 1 Corinthians 6:19b-20; 2 Corinthians 6:21). Does one thank God by severing himself from the body—by refusing to be his brother's or sister's helper?

Would one say the same thing regarding other aspects of life? For example, would one say, "I don't have to go to school (elementary through university) to be educated?" While it is true that some have been educated outside of schools and colleges, they have not done so on their own. Education requires social interaction with others. Teachers, parents, and peers are essential in the learning process.

One can be a member of some social fraternity or professional organization and not participate, but I know of few who derive any benefit from them who are not involved in some kind of dialogue at the local, state, or national level.

To use another analogy, Tim, how many people in sports—tennis, golf, baseball, basketball, football, or skiing—do you know who are not members of some group? I still remember when you wanted to take tennis lessons, how you insisted that you had to do more than practice to become a pro. You said you had to have lessons from a pro— and you were right! If people in fraternal and professional organizations, and in sports, feel that participation and instruction are essential, why do some professing Christians or those on the fringes think that they can sever themselves from the body of Christ and live? Either one is a part of the body of which Christ is the head, or he is not (Colossians 1:18, 22; 2:10; 1 Corinthians 12:12-13, 27).

Our Lord used the allegory of the vine and the branches to illustrate the essential unity a believer must maintain with his Lord (John 15:1-17). If the branch (the believer) is a part of the vine (Christ), then it lives, grows, is pruned and cared for, and bears fruit. If the branch is cut off from the vine, it dies.

Tim, I really think it is often a combination of things that keeps people away from church. Going to church and participating actively involves acknowledging that one has needs and "can't make it on his own." This is difficult for many to do. Some refuse to acknowledge that they are weak, finite, and in need of forgiveness, reconciliation, and divine assistance. Pride gets in the way.

Also some are self-righteous. They feel they are better than "those hypocrites in the church." This is really a defense mechanism, an attempt to divert attention from one's own shortcomings and negative qualities by pointing the finger at others. It's a matter of "log jumping"—jumping over the log in one's own eye to use the magnifying glass to see the splinter of wood in someone else's (Matthew 7:3-5). My response, in essence, is this: "If you are not hypocritical, if you are indeed so virtuous, come, show us the way!" It takes humility, as well as compassion for others, to take one's place in a Christian community to serve and to be served. There is a natural reluctance not to make oneself vulnerable. "True confession may be good for the soul," but some cannot bring themselves to admit that they have sinned and done things that are wrong. It takes a big person to admit that he needs help.

For the Christian there is no salvation outside the church, the body of Christ. This interpretation is based on the teaching of Christ. He not only said that the church is made up of all who confess that he is the Christ, the Son of God. He also insisted that the royal law of the kingdom is to love one's neighbor as one loves himself (Matthew 16:13-18; John 14:6; 8:31-32; Mark 12:31; James 2:8). John includes more of our Lord's words that give an added dimension to the command: "That you love one another as I have loved you" (John 15:12).

If we profess to believe in God but then refuse to affiliate with the body of Christ and minister to those in it, as well as those without, we make a mockery of the concept of faith or belief (1 John 3:17; 4:20-21; James 2:14-17, 26). The apostle James adds that there is only one kind of faith that God honors and that is obedient faith—not intellectual assent (faith), per se. He says, "You believe that there is only one God? Good! The demons also believe—and tremble with fear" (2:19, TEV). It's not belief alone, but active belief, faith expressed sincerely, honestly, without hypocrisy, that God honors. In addition, good works must be done from a pure motive (Philippians 2:3; Matthew 7:21-23).

So then, Tim, participation in the church is not an option for the Christian. It is the place (1) where we demonstrate the sincerity of our faith through worship; (2) where we are nurtured in the faith; and (3) where we minister to the needs of others in the body of Christ. It is also the continuing incarnation of Christ in the world. Through the church God reaches out to serve a needy world.

Furthermore, Tim, the church is where ministers and teachers proclaim the Word of God, interpret it, and apply it to our lives. It is also where we participate in the Christian ordinances of baptism, marriage, and the Lord's Supper. (Some denominations refer to these as sacraments.)

Hearing the Word of God preached is a must for the Christian, because the Word is a "living" thing and by hearing the Word we are nurtured in the faith (Hebrews 4:12;

Romans 10:17). As Paul said to Timothy, the Word "is useful for teaching the truth, rebuking error, correcting faults, and giving instruction for right living..." (2 Timothy 3:16, TEV; see Romans 15:4; John 17:17; Acts 20:32).

When we hear the Word, the Holy Spirit speaks to us, either confirming or condemning our thoughts and/or behavior (Ephesians 6:17; 2 Timothy 3:15-17; John 17:17; Hebrews 4:12; Romans 2:15).

While the Roman Catholic Church has seven sacraments, many Protestants identify two as instituted by Christ in the Gospels. Both Catholics and Protestants agree that the most crucial observances are baptism and communion. Baptism marks our initiation into the church. It is a sign and seal of our engrafting into the body of Christ. We do not participate in baptism to be saved—God did that for us in Christ. It serves as an outward sign of an invisible, inward work of grace. By participating in the act of baptism, the Christian is witnessing to those inside and outside the church that he has received God's forgiveness in Christ. The act symbolizes that in Christ we have died to sin and been raised to newness of life in him (Romans 6:3-4; 8:11), that we have experienced Christ's transforming power and have decided to walk in the way of Christ (John 14:6; Acts 9:2). The baptismal ceremony is a joyful one, somewhat similar to the joyful celebration of marriage. As the bride and groom become one flesh, so the Christian becomes one with the body of Christ.

Foot washing, while not classified as a sacrament, is often associated with the "love feast" and communion. It is regarded by many Christians as an ordinance—a meaningful rite and symbolic ritual. Our Lord introduced this in the upper room before the shared meal or love feast prior to the "Lord's supper" (John 13:1-20). Foot washing symbolizes the Christian's servant role. While this ordinance is regularly observed by churches in the Anabaptist tradition (Mennonite, Brethren, etc.), some in other denominations, such as the United Methodists and Roman Catholics, are increasingly adopting this ordinance.

The second sacrament the church shares is the Lord's supper, or holy communion. Many refer to the communion service as a Eucharistic service, that is, the giving of thanks to God for our redemption in Christ. This sacrament was instituted by our Lord prior to his death (Mark 14:22-26; 1 Corinthians 11:23-30). The bread and the wine are visible symbols of our Lord's broken body and shed blood on our behalf. It is at this service that we experience the unique presence of Christ as the Holy Spirit ministers to us (Luke 24:28-35; 1 Corinthians 10:16-17).

Communion, more than any other observance, reminds us that salvation is something that God did in Christ. It is not something we can earn or do for ourselves. Therefore, Tim, never refrain from taking communion because you do not "feel worthy." Of course, we should confess all known sins prior to taking communion, and ask forgiveness of those we have offended—seeking reconciliation. But then we can take communion with the assurance that in Christ we are forgiven. Actually only those who "feel worthy" should abstain from taking communion, for apparently they have missed the whole point that Christ died for sinners, and Christians are sinners, too. In addition, communion points us to the ultimate triumph of God in Christ at his second coming. For as Paul said, "As often as you eat this bread and drink the cup, you proclaim the Lord's death until he comes" (1 Corinthians 11:26, RSV).

Finally, Tim, God expects the church to be his servant *in* the world. In our Lord's high priestly prayer he says the servant's place is out in the world where the needs are (John

17:11, 15; Matthew 25:31-46; 22:4-10; 28:19-20; Acts 1:6-8). He cautions us, however, not to be *of* the world (John 17:15; 2 John 2:15-17). We are not to live its lifestyle. The world is concerned with exercising power over others; that is how worldly people measure success (Mark 19:42-43). But not so the church. We are to be imitators of Christ who took a towel and assumed the servant's role (Mark 10:44; John 13:12-17). Only when we minister to human need, not only to those in the church, but also to those whom others have rejected, those who cannot help themselves, and those who cannot "return the favor," are we imitating Christ (Matthew 24:45-51; 25:14-30; Luke 14:12-14).

Summing up, Tim, the church is composed of all believers. It is the body of Christ. Christ is its head. Our life and growth in Christ calls for continuous involvement in the church through participation in a local church, a believing community. If we sever our connection with the church, we cut ourselves off from Christ, from the preaching of the Word, the sacraments or ordinances, and the responsibilities we have toward those in the fellowship.

Our Lord is the vine. As branches of the vine, we must abide in him to be fruitful. Our Lord calls us to imitate him by performing a servant role. Active involvement in the church is not an option. It is a must. Just as life in any other organization requires active participation, so we as Christians must participate in the life of the church. As servants we not only witness by word to the gospel, but we minister to the walking wounded, those who are hurting among us. As the servant church, Tim, we exist for others.

Until the next letter, then, take care of yourself. God be with you.

With all my love,
Dad

The Second Coming of Christ

Dear Tim,

I want to write you a letter about the second coming of Christ, not only because it is part of our Christian hope, but because there are so many conflicting interpretations of it.

As Christians we believe that Christ will come in triumph over the forces of evil (1 Corinthians 15:20-28). We believe that at his appearing Christians will be ushered into the blessings of the life to come (1 Thessalonians 4:13-18; 1 John 3:2; 1 Peter 4:13; 1 Corinthians 15:50-57). Those who have died in Christ, together with those living at his return, will share the joy and blessings that will be realized when the body of Christ is complete (1 Thessalonians 4:16-18; Hebrews 11:40).

It is difficult to be specific about the end of the world or the second coming of Christ, because our Lord himself said: "No one knows about that day or hour, not even the angels in heaven, nor the Son, but only the Father" (Mark 13:32; Matthew 24:36-39; 25:13; Acts 1:7; 2 Thessalonians 5:2; 1 Timothy 6:15; 2 Peter 3:10; Revelation 3:3).

The main eschatological discourses in the Gospels (those dealing with the second coming) were grouped by the evangelists in Mark 13, Matthew 24, and Luke 21. However, many other parables and sayings of Jesus deal with the "appearing of the Son of Man"—another expression used in the New Testament for the second coming (1 Timothy 6:13-16; 2 Timothy 4:1, 8; Titus 2:13). The chapters dealing with the "end" and the second coming are not easy to interpret. Biblical scholars have wrestled with these for centuries. Although there is a consensus of opinion and interpretation on the main concepts, students of the Bible do not agree on details. Most, however, would agree with T. W. Manson (a scholar of international repute) who concluded in his book on *The Teachings of Jesus* that the one thing we can affirm with confidence is that Jesus taught, and the apostles believed, that he would in fact come again. The evidence is set forth in the Gospels and the rest of the New Testament.

Undoubtedly you wonder why some churches and groups seem to be preoccupied with predicting the precise time of the end. Some are convinced that they know exactly what historical events will occur before Christ returns. Whenever Russia, China, Israel, or one of the other Middle East nations "sneezes," these prophetic predictors stand ready to tell us specifically what it means in the end-time scheme of things.

Furthermore, these same prophetic "experts" talk a great deal about "the last days," and "the signs of the times." Yet our Lord said that the catastrophes and crises they point to as marking the coming of the end are only the beginning of "birth pangs or pains" (Mark 13:8). The expression "birth pangs of the Messiah" was a familiar expression to the Jews. They used it to refer to the "time of trouble" (wars, persecution, oppression, and cataclysms in nature—earthquakes, etc.) which they believed would precede the coming of the Messiah. Here our Lord uses the concept of "birth pangs" in connection with his second coming.

Interestingly, in the book of Acts, Luke clearly affirms the early church's belief that the "last days" the prophet Joel spoke of had already come (Acts 2:14-25; Hebrews 1:2). We too are living in the last days—the days blessed by the realization of salvation wrought by God in Christ, days in which God is present in a unique way by his Spirit.

But you'll find, Tim, that the apostles also used the expression "last day" and "last time" in a futuristic sense (2 Timothy 3:1; 1 Peter 1:5; 2 Peter 3:3; 1 John 2:18; Jude 18). Furthermore, our Lord and the apostles also spoke about "that day," referring to the last day, the day of judgment at the end of history (Matthew 7:22; Luke 10:12; John 14:20; 2 Timothy 1:12; 4:18). What we have here, therefore, is a combination of a cyclical and linear view of history. The "last days" of Joel were indeed fulfilled when Christ came the first time. But between the first and second coming, there are many ages or cycles filled with both pain and blessing. There are many cycles, but in God's own time one of these cycles will be the last. This interpretation makes sense to me. I hope it does to you.

Well, Tim, what are we to make of those who predict the end? You've heard the expression, "Fools rush in where angels fear to tread." I'm afraid that is what we have in this situation. When the apostle Paul was witnessing to King Agrippa about Christ, Festus (a Roman ruler in Judea) said: "Paul, you are mad; your great learning is turning you mad" (Acts 26:24, RSV). Unfortunately, in the case of many of those who chart the end-times with such specificity, it's a case of "a little knowledge being a dangerous thing." Dr. W. D. Chamberlain, my New Testament professor at Louisville Presbyterian Seminary, used to say, "People speak loudest about that which they know least." I'm afraid this is the case with predictors of the end times.

I find it difficult to understand why some who speak so much about the authority of the Bible refuse to submit to its authority. Instead, they defy their Lord who clearly taught that no one knows when he will return. Why do they do this? There probably are several reasons. In many cases the individuals were led to Christ through such a group and they have merely adopted their beliefs. Others, consciously or subconsciously, are so obsessed with the *next* world that they get involved in charting the end of this one. It is a way of escaping their responsibility of serving Christ in this world. Still others derive a sense of status by claiming to know the unknowable. They are modern *gnostics* (from the Greek word meaning "to know" or "have knowledge"). Gnostic was the name given to early Christian sects whose members prided themselves as being God's elect to whom he had revealed some special knowledge from which the nonelect were excluded.

There have always been those who have predicted the end, Tim. In the church of Thessalonica Paul had to deal with a group who said that the second coming had already taken place (2 Thessalonians 2:1-2). Before, during, and after the Protestant Reformation there were well-meaning, oppressed groups who desperately longed for Christ's return. They looked for deliverance from political oppression and abject poverty to the bliss of heaven. But despite their sincerity, they were misguided and wrong. North America seems to have more than its share of sects who make the imminent return of Christ the focus of their thinking and witnessing, rather than the good news of salvation associated with his first advent.

Charles Taze Russell, who founded the Jehovah's Witnesses, claimed that Christ had returned *invisibly* in 1874. (That was clever, wasn't it?) He also predicted the end in

1914. A classic group of adventists were the Millerites. William Miller of Lowell Hampton, New York, predicted the Lord's return by March 21, 1844. But he didn't come. Then one of his disciples, John Couch, recalculated "prophetic utterances of the Old Testament" and predicted the end would come on October 22, 1844. These Christians didn't plant crops; they gave away their money and disposed of their businesses. But the day came and went and Christ did not return. Tim, libraries have scores of books recounting the frustrated hopes of sects that desperately longed for, and predicted, the end.

The thing that makes it so tragic is that the Spirit of God and Christ does dwell within us now. In fact, Tim, we are in the kingdom now (1 John 3:2). As I mentioned earlier, the rule or reign of God is a spiritual experience, and as Paul states so clearly, to be "in Christ" is to be "in the kingdom" (Acts 20:21, 25; 28:31; 2 Corinthians 5:17; Philippians 1:1, *et al.*). The apostle John, however, equates "having eternal life" and "life" with "being in the kingdom" (John 3:16; 10:10). Unfortunately, many, like the "elder brother" in the parable of the prodigal son, never claim the blessings of the kingdom that Christ died to give us (Luke 15:25-32; Acts 2:36-39).

Many lonely people who crave friendship and a sense of belonging fall prey to these "blind leaders of the blind." Ironically, our Lord warns us that many will come claiming to have "special knowledge," and even claiming to be the Christ. But says Jesus, "Do not believe it. For false Christs and false prophets will appear and perform signs to deceive even the elect—if possible. So be on your guard; I have told you everything ahead of time" (Mark 13:21-23).

I guess it is natural for Christians to ask the same questions skeptics asked of the apostle Peter. "Where is the promise of his coming? For . . . all things have continued as they were from the beginning of creation." Peter answered that they "ignore this one fact, beloved, that with the Lord one day is as a thousand years, and a thousand years as one day. The Lord is not slow about his promise as some count slowness, but is forbearing toward you, not wishing that any should perish, but that all should reach repentance" (2 Peter 3:4, 8-9, RSV). So, while non-Christians should view the delay in the Lord's return to usher in the fullness of the kingdom as an opportunity to repent, we Christians should view it as an opportunity to witness.

Tim, let me mention a point that our Lord stressed repeatedly. He said that it's our duty to "watch," that is, "be alert" and active in his service. He clearly spells this out in terms of honesty, industry, compassion, and fairness in our interpersonal relationships (Matthew 24:42-51).

Our Lord asks, "Can any of you live a bit longer [or grow a bit taller] by worrying about it?" (Matthew 6:27, TEV). And I would ask, "Can anyone hasten the return of Christ by indulging in fancy guesswork?" God is not going to judge us on our ability to guess the date of the end. He is going to judge us on the basis of our behavior—how we used our abilities and resources in relationship to the needs of others. The parables (the sheep and the goats, the talents, the ten virgins, the wedding garment, the sower, the wheat and the weeds, the unforgiving servant, the rich man and Lazarus, the Pharisee and the tax collector, the good Samaritan) all emphasize that behavior either validates or invalidates our profession. The apostles make this point in their epistles.

Still you will meet Christians, well-meaning and serious ones, who will insist that the signs of the times all point to the fact that the "battle of Armageddon" is shaping up and is imminent (Revelation 16:16). (Armageddon comes from the Hebrew *Har-Magedon,* literally the "Hill of Megiddo," the site of numerous battles between Israel and her foes.) Armageddon has become a symbol of the final conflict between the forces of good and evil—God and Satan. As you know, Tim, my doctoral dissertation dealt with this entire question of the end (eschatology) that includes the messianic hope, the idea of a final conflict, the messianic age, as well as heaven and hell. I studied both the literature of the Old Testament, the Apocrypha, the Pseudepigrapha, the Dead Sea Scrolls, as well as the literature of the New Testament. It was a rewarding and painful five-year experience. It was painful because my research compelled me to part with some of the ideas I had been taught as a young person, ideas such as those we've been talking about.

What I found was that the idea of an earthly final conflict between Israel and her foes tends to give way to a spiritual conflict between God and Satan. And the New Testament, the Gospels and the Epistles, supports the fact that the "decisive battle" took place at the cross (Acts 4:23-31; 1 Corinthians 2:6-8; Colossians 1:13-15; 1:19-20; Ephesians 2:15-17). It was there that God in Christ decisively defeated Satan and the forces of evil (Hebrews 2:14-15). The resurrection and ascension authenticate that victory (Philippians 2:5-11; 1 Timothy 3:16; Acts 2:32-36). God has not only set us free from the power of Satan, sin, and death, but he has given us his Holy Spirit who bears witness with our spirit that we are his children (Romans 8:16; Galatians 4:6). The second coming is assured by virtue of Christ's victory at the cross. The end, in a sense, was moved up to the middle—the cross. Our eternal destiny is not decided at the end of our lives at the judgment, but now by our response to Christ (John 3:18).

The idea of a battle of Armageddon is mentioned in the New Testament only in the book of Revelation. As I suggested in an earlier letter, Revelation is a highly symbolic book. The symbols should not be taken literally, but we, should look for the meaning behind the symbolism. What the symbolism of Revelation says clearly is that in times of trouble our Lord comes to be with us—to comfort, strengthen, and deliver us. He decisively defeated Satan and the forces of evil in his first advent and at his second advent will usher in the fullness of the kingdom. While Christians differ on the details, virtually all agree with the basic interpretation above.

Let me say a word about judgment, Tim, because this is associated with the end. While it is definitely true that there will be a final judgment (Matthew 25:31-45; 2 Corinthians 5:10; 1 Corinthians 4:5; 2 Timothy 4:1; Hebrews 9:27; 1 Peter 4:5; Revelation 20:11-15), we are also judged by God daily. As Paul says, when we think or act, God speaks to us through our conscience and either confirms us if we are right or accuses us if we are wrong (Romans 2:15). Furthermore, Paul urges us to judge ourselves (1 Corinthians 11:31). In addition, we are admonished to submit to God's judgment now (1 Corinthians 4:4; 11:32). If we do not modify our behavior in the light of God's truth that comes to us through reading the Bible, through the preaching of the Word, through family, friends, and the like, then we bring the greater judgment of God on us.

Therefore, Tim, it's important for us to be open to the influence of God's Spirit, and not shut his voice out of our minds and hearts (1 Corinthians 2:9-16; 1 Thessalonians 5:19). We must allow him to lead us in the ways of Christ.

What about the second coming of Christ, then? As believers we affirm with confidence the teaching of our Lord and his apostles that at God's appointed time Jesus Christ will come again. At that time both those who have died in Christ and those who are alive at his coming will share in the fullness of the kingdom. While there are those who try to predict the exact time of his coming, Jesus warned us against wasting precious time and energy trying to second-guess God. Jesus said that even he didn't know the time of the end—only God knows. It is our responsibility to live and share the good news of Christ's first coming with those who have never heard of him.

God judges us daily, as well as at the end of history. On that day, he will reward us not for our ability to guess the end time, but for faithful stewardship. Scripture teaches that the decisive battle with the forces of evil took place at the cross. We are, therefore, living in the last days. We are now sharing in the kingdom that our Lord ushered in, but we look forward to the second coming—that day when the kingdom will be fully realized.

Tim, while I am grateful for the blessed hope of heaven and the peace of heart and mind that hope gives to us, I must confess that I am thoroughly enjoying the blessings of God's kingdom now. Christ's Spirit indwells us now (John 20:22; Galatians 4:6; Ephesians 1:13; 1 Corinthians 3:16; 2 Timothy 1:7-14). In times of crisis and of need he comes to us with special strength, comfort, and help. He sustains us through all the changing circumstances of life. When we die, we have confidence that he will receive us (Philippians 1:21-23; 2 Corinthians 5:8; Colossians 1:27). What more could anyone ask? Nevertheless, God in Christ will return and usher in the fullness of the kingdom at some future date. "Even so, come, Lord Jesus."

Keep the faith, Tim.

All my love,
Dad

Christianity and Other Religions

Dear Tim,

When mom and I visited you at Ocean City, New Jersey, you told us about a group who called themselves the "Restored Israel." The members you met said that their leader was the resurrected Jeremiah, but at the present time he was in hiding because the FBI was after him for tax evasion! I read some of the literature they gave you, which seemed to be a curious mixture of fact and fiction. You'll find that most heresies contain a mixture of truth and error. At that time, I decided to write to you about Christianity and other religions, including contemporary sects.

Tim, I want to begin by saying that the best defense against error is a knowledge of the truth. But having said that, I realize that this is what the members of sects and non-Christian religions say also, and they also claim to have "the truth." Therefore, it is not enough to merely claim that the Bible contains the true revelation of God to man. Nonetheless, this is where the Christian begins, with the Scriptures of the Old and New Testaments as his authoritative guide. The Bible is our infallible rule of faith and practice. It is the frame of reference against which we judge the beliefs of other religions and philosophies (2 Timothy 3:16; 2 Peter 1:20-21).

Furthermore, it is not enough to resort to the Scriptures alone to check various beliefs and practices as the Bereans did, for many sects use the Scriptures to support their beliefs (Acts 17:10-11). We must interpret Scripture within its historical and social context. We must check our interpretation against the consensus of Christian scholarship within the church. As I mentioned in my second letter, if any individual comes forward with some startling "new truth" that runs counter to what the church has held in the past, you can be fairly certain that it is heretical. I know, Tim, that there have been Augustines, Luthers, Wesleys, and Galileos—but even they were authenticated by other scholars. The point I'm making is, check a teaching out carefully before you "buy it."

I know that it is considered arbitrary and narrow-minded by some standards, but of necessity there can be only *one* true, complete revelation of the nature and will of God—and that is in Christ (Hebrews 1:1-3; 1 Timothy 2:5; Ephesians 4:4-5; 1 Corinthians 8:4-6). Occasionally you may be asked, "If God revealed himself in Jesus Christ, why hasn't he done it again in another person?" I like the answer G. Campbell Morgan gave. He said that since God made a full and final revelation of himself in Jesus Christ, there is no need for him to make any others.

Tim, Paul was convinced that Christ was the only saving revelation God has made. In his letter to the Galatians he said:

> But even if we or an angel from heaven should preach a gospel other than the one we preached to you, let him be eternally condemned! As we have already said, so now I say again: If anybody is preaching to you a gospel other than what you accepted, let him be eternally condemned (1:8-9).

He leaves no room for doubt. "For there is one God and one mediator between God and men, the man Christ Jesus, who gave himself as a ransom for all men—the testimony given in its proper time" (1 Timothy 2:5; Galatians 4:4). There is only *one* Gospel, only *one* way of salvation. It is a gift we receive. It is not something that we can earn. "Good deeds" are a result of regeneration, not a prerequisite. Good works are a part of our grateful response to the free gift of God (Titus 2:14; Ephesians 2:8-10).

Where, then, does this leave other religions? How do they relate to Christianity? Well, Tim, there is a relationship, and yet there isn't.

On the one hand, non-Christian religions contain elements of truth in them—just as contemporary sects do. The apostle Paul acknowledged this, as can be seen in his exchange with the Greeks at Mars Hill in Athens:

> Paul then stood up in the meeting of the Areopagus and said: "Men of Athens! I see that in every way you are very religious. For as I walked around and observed your objects of worship, I even found an altar with this inscription: TO AN UNKNOWN GOD. Now what you worship as something unknown I am going to proclaim to you" (Acts 17:22-23).

He didn't say: "You ignorant, benighted Athenians, your religion is *all* wrong! I will condescend to set you straight!" No, he recognized what truth they had and related the gospel to it. Read the entire speech—it's a masterpiece.

On the other hand, non-Christian religions, as well as sects, do not compare with orthodox Christianity at all. They do not lead the adherent into a full experience with God (Acts 4:12). They do not offer forgiveness and reconciliation (Ephesians 1:7-8). They do not offer regeneration—a new birth—in this life (2 Corinthians 5:17; Titus 3:5). They do not offer the hope of life everlasting (John 3:16; 11:25-26). They do not offer a yoke which is relatively easy to bear (Matthew 11:28-30). They do not place on their followers the same responsibilities for others inside and outside of their "church" (Galatians 6:2; Luke 10:25-37).

In Christianity there is no *karma* (the doctrine that one's rebirth after death is determined by the thoughts, words, and deeds done in this life). There is no denial of life, no escaping the problems that confront individuals and society. God is not identified with the physical world of nature, but separate from it. The world of nature is ours to enjoy—although God expects us to reverence all life and to live in harmony within our natural environment.

Why, then, do we have these other religions? How did they originate? Paul attributes the rise of non-Christian religions to mankind's rebellion against God—a result of the fall. In Romans he says that the revelation of God to man was, and is, visible in nature. There is a natural revelation of God not only in the world of nature, but also within the human heart/mind (Romans 1:21-32). Man, however, rebelled against God, rejecting both the revelation and the intuitive knowledge he had. In place of this, he developed religions that permitted him to satisfy his egoistic desires, both of the flesh and the mind.

I might add, Tim, that individuals create new sects and cults out of their own felt needs, as well as out of ignorance. And yes, many are started by charlatans out to make a fast buck. Furthermore, new movements and revivals often spring up within mainline denominations because people's needs are not being met. Church leaders and even theological seminaries get out of touch; they fail to perceive the real needs of people. Often the simple gospel—the basic Christian message—becomes so commonplace to them they fail to realize there are millions in North America who do not really know *who* Jesus is and *why* he came. Within the last two hundred years or so one could cite the Methodist Church, the Salvation Army, and the charismatic movements as excellent examples of newly formed denominations and movements that have grown out of regular denominations.

Many find it difficult to accept Paul's argument that God's revelation was plain for people to see, and that monotheism preceded polytheism. But Samuel M. Zwemer, once a missionary to the Muslims, and a professor of the history of religion and missions at Princeton Theological Seminary, on the basis of a lifetime of research, corroborates Paul's thesis.

It was from a world that had degenerated into polytheism that God called Abraham to be the father of the Hebrew people. Subsequently, he called Moses, led the children of Israel out of Egypt, welded them into a nation at Mt. Sinai, and under Joshua's leadership helped them occupy the land of Palestine. Through Israel God mediated his special revelation to the nations that surrounded her. Then, as I have mentioned several times previously, his full and complete revelation was channeled to all mankind through Jesus Christ (2 Corinthians 4:6; Hebrews 1:1-3; Colossians 1:19).

What of other religions then—Judaism, Buddhism, Hinduism, Islam, and others? Are they not equally valid? Don't all rivers lead into the sea? Don't all religions lead to God? Don't all say substantially the same thing? Don't all offer the same salvation?

It's strange, Tim, that in every other field of endeavor you will never hear people say that "it all depends on how you look at it." Does $2 + 2 = 4$? Could it be that $3 + 4 = 4$ or $0 + 1 = 4$? Does H_2O give us water? Could it be O_2H? Was the First World War fought in 1914-18, or was it 1920-24? It's really ridiculous to ask questions like this, isn't it? Yet people make absurd statements about religion, and especially Christianity, insisting that there is no one true religion, that all are equally valid.

There is truth and falsehood in science and history. There is good and bad art. There is good and bad music. It doesn't depend on how one looks at it! Everyone is entitled to his opinion, but everyone's opinion is not equally valid.

I believe there is truth and falsehood in religion, and that there is only one true religion. All religions cannot be true. That notion is self-contradictory. My conviction that Christianity is true is not only based on faith; it makes sense. It is reasonable and logical. Furthermore, because the Christian system of belief is true, it works—not vice versa.

I mentioned earlier that we need to do more than claim biblical authority for our beliefs. Another way one can show the authenticity of Christianity is by looking at the life and teachings of those who established the various religions. When you compare them (Buddha, Muhammad, *et al.*) with Jesus, they pale into insignificance. Jesus affirmed life; he didn't deny it. He practiced love and justice; he didn't just talk about it. He was holy, even as he associated with the unholy; he did not practice holiness in isolation. His teachings, when truly internalized and practiced, not only result in self-fulfillment, but also in a sense of community that cannot be equaled. The benevolent and humanitarian efforts of the Christian church are unmatched by any other religion.

Only in Christianity does one find a God who seeks man. God is not a bogyman to be feared, but one who offers forgiveness in Jesus Christ (John 3:17). Jesus taught that salvation is not some far off distant hope, but a present experience of deliverance and renewal (Luke 24:46-49).

Only the Christian church has given her sons and daughters, as well as her substance, to minister throughout the world in relief (food and clothing), medical, educational, agricultural, technical, and evangelistic programs.

I know there are those who say: "But what of the Inquisition, the witch hunts, etc.?" One doesn't judge a movement by what its worst adherents have done. Those demonstrations of "man's inhumanity to man" were unforgivable, as were the justifications of slavery by both the African blacks who cooperated with whites in enslaving their brothers and sisters, and those who justified it on our own shores. One might also point to the church's spread of Western culture as an accompaniment to Christianity. But really, Tim, no objective review of past history could deny the fact that wherever the Christian faith has been truly proclaimed and practiced, the general condition of the people has been greatly uplifted. Furthermore, a clear distinction must be drawn between genuine Christianity and that erroneously associated with soldiers, sailors, and businessmen who have gone out from "Christian" nations.

I might add that the track record of surrogate religions is extremely atrocious by comparison. We have lived through enough of the so-called "people's revolutions" or "liberation movements" in Russia, China, Cuba, and Africa to realize that the workers have lost more than their chains. They have lost their individual freedom and millions have lost their lives. They may have gained a full stomach, but they have lost their souls. You have only to read *One Day in the Life of Ivan Denisovich* or *Gulag Archipelago*, by Aleksandr Solzhenitsyn, to realize this. Surrogate religions, such as communism, fascism, and other forms of totalitarianism that have been established in this century, have given us an incomparable record of barbarity, brutality, and genocide. Who could match the godless brutality and butchering of Stalin, Hitler, or Idi Amin?

And still people persist in saying, "Just so you have faith, that's all that matters! All religions are the same." Are they now? Ask the man whose daughter was drawn into the Children of God sect, and from whom he has not heard in over a year, if all religions are the same. Ask young people who have managed to break away from the Moonies if all religions are the same. Ask the relatives and survivors of the People's Temple sect of Jonesville, Guyana, if all religions are the same.

No, Tim, *what* and *whom* one has faith in is crucial. And the Christ factor is the crucial one—the key. He is the one who really sets mankind free!

But I guess it's logical to ask, if Christ is the one true revelation of God, what of those who have never heard the gospel? Are they without hope—completely estranged from God? Are they lost? Tim, let me separate these questions and relate them (1) to Christians and the church, and (2) to those who have never heard the gospel.

First of all, it is not only the responsibility of ministers within the church to share the gospel, but it is the responsibility and privilege of each believer to do so (Matthew 28:19-20; Acts 1:8; 2 Timothy 2:2; 1 Peter 3:15). But people cannot respond to a gospel which they have never heard (Romans 10:13-15; Acts 17:16-34; 19:1-7; 1 Corinthians 15:34). Nonetheless, the non-Christian is far from being completely estranged, or cut off from God. As Paul said, "In him we live and move and have our being" (Acts 17:28). Just as those living before Christ who were not believers (had no knowledge of the God of Israel) were recipients of God's common grace, so those outside of Christ and the church today are also recipients (Matthew 5:43-48). Further-

170

more, Tim, the image of God which we possess was not completely destroyed by the fall. This means that God can and does communicate with man—the unbeliever and the believer (Acts 2:37-45; 4:4; 8:34-38; 9:1-19). Therefore, even though man outside of Christ may be immersed in a pagan religion or a religious surrogate such as secularism, he can be reached by the Spirit of God and the gospel.

The apostle Paul speaks of a natural revelation of God, as well as an innate sense of morality. This not only means that all men can know God, but it also means that they have an innate sense of right and wrong which convicts them when they do wrong (Romans 2:12-16). But Paul is not content to leave men in this paradoxical condition of knowing right from wrong but being powerless to do anything about it (Romans 7:7-25; 10:13-15). He feels that it is his responsibility and ours to share the light with those who are in darkness (Acts 13:47; Romans 1:14; 1 Corinthians 9:16; Matthew 28:19-20).

Jesus is "the way and the truth and the life," and no one can approach the Father except through him (John 14:6). The truth here is crystal clear—one can only be saved through Christ. But it seems to me, Tim, that here our Lord is offering himself to his contemporaries as the way to the Father. Therefore, if Christ is to become the way to God today for our contemporaries, then we must share the good news. Just as a cancer cure cannot possibly help someone who has never been told of it and never had the opportunity to receive it, so Christ cannot become the way for those who have never heard of him or been offered the gospel (Mark 5:28; John 5:1-14; Acts 9:34; Romans 10:14).

Now, second, let me briefly address the question, "What of those who have never heard? What will happen to them? Are they lost? Are they cut off from the grace and mercy of

God?" The answer is a yes and a no. No in the sense, as I mentioned earlier, that all peoples are recipients of God's common grace. But yes in the sense that they have not been privileged to hear and respond to the gospel which alone is able to make them whole. While they know about God and are without excuse, they cannot possibly live up to the righteous demands of God because of their "fallen state." Therefore, I see two classes of lost individuals—those who have never heard, and those who have rejected the gospel after having had the opportunity to hear and understand. Each group will be judged by a just and loving God who will treat each individual within those groups according to the opportunities he has had to hear and respond to the gospel (Luke 12:47-48).

Frankly, Tim, I can't understand the reasoning of those who say that the motivation for missions or evangelism will be undermined if we say God will treat those who have never heard the gospel with love and compassion, as well as with equity. Some will say, "Well, if God will deal mercifully and justly with those who have never heard, why go tell them of Christ? For if they reject him they will definitely be lost! If we don't go, at least they may have a chance."

Tim, I think that kind of response betrays a partial, if not basic, misunderstanding of the gospel. As I mentioned earlier, the good news is that we can know the redeeming, liberating power of Christ now, in this life. (This truth in no way minimizes the Christian's conviction that he will continue to live and serve God in the life to come.) That is why we share Christ! It is our responsibility to share the gospel. How individuals respond is their responsibility. One wouldn't fault or blame a physician for offering medicine to cure cancer, arguing that he shouldn't do this because some will not accept or use the medication and, therefore, die.

There are Christians who believe that those who have never heard will suffer forever in hell. But I feel that C. S. Lewis' statement more accurately reflects what we know of the God revealed in Christ and the mood of Scripture. He said: "But the truth is God has not told us what his arrangements about the other people are. We do know that no man can be saved except through Christ; we do not know that only those who know him can be saved through him."

Tim, Scripture does not unequivocally tell us how God will deal with those who have never heard. Therefore, it's best not to speculate. Long ago Abraham asked: "Shall not the Judge of all the earth do right?" (Genesis 18:25, RSV). He will!

Therefore, we Christians must go, and/or we must support with our money and prayers those who take the gospel to others. We must do this for at least three reasons. First, because we have experienced new life in Christ it's natural to want to share him with others (2 Kings 7:9; John 1:40-43; 4:29-30). Second, it is our obligation. It is the only way we have of expressing our gratitude to God and to those who shared Christ with us (Romans 1:14; 1 Corinthians 9:16). Third, Christ has commanded us to go and tell the good news (Matthew 28:18-20; John 20:21-23; Acts 1:6-8).

So while Scripture does not clearly state what will happen to those who have never heard, it is clear about the fate of those who have willfully rejected the gospel. They, along with those who are insincere in their profession, are lost (John 3:18-21; Matthew 7:21-23; 25:31-45; 2 Thessalonians 1:7-10; James 2:26; 1 John 4:20-21). It matters not whether one is a refined, cultured, intellectual pagan or a ruthless member of organized crime—if he rejects God's love and law he is lost. Heaven wouldn't be heaven if the unconverted exploiter and oppressor were there. Neither would it be fair if God compelled those who wanted to go to hell, to go to heaven. C. S. Lewis illustrated this tragic truth beautifully in his book, *The Great Divorce*.

Tim, when you share this answer with some, they may object and ask, "How can a God of love send anyone to hell?" Of course the answer is that God doesn't send anyone to hell. Each individual decides his own destiny by his response to God's offer of salvation in Christ. We decide whether it will be heaven or hell.

Some who find the doctrine of God's justice difficult to accept believe that eventually God will redeem everyone. In this way they hope to save God from "character assassination." But if God were going to redeem all, why would he wait until the next life? Why not do it before such happenings as the Stalin purges, the Polish pogroms. Hitler's Dachau and Auschwitz, Japan's Pearl Harbor, and America's Hiroshima and Nagasaki?

As much as I wish there were no hell, I'm afraid there is— love and justice demand it.

So, Tim, we share Christ because he has redeemed us. He has made us whole. Therefore, we want others to know this same wholeness. What God will do with people who have never heard, I don't know. I only know that "the Judge of all the earth will do right!"

Let me sum things up for you, Tim. We Christians believe that the full and final revelation of God was made in Jesus Christ. This revelation is mediated to us through the Scriptures, as the Holy Spirit leads us into a saving knowledge of God through Christ. While other religions contain religious truths, only in Christ do we find God's saving truth. While God called Israel to be his servant and to be a light to the nations, only in Christ, his Suffering Servant, was this role fully realized and salvation accomplished and offered to all mankind. God has commissioned us to carry the light of the gospel into all the world.

Just as there is truth and falsehood in science, so there is in religion. We believe that Christianity is the true religion. It is the only religion that portrays God as one who seeks man, offering forgiveness, reconciliation, and a new life through fellowship with Christ and his church. Furthermore, the founder of our religion (humanly speaking), Jesus Christ, excels all other religious founders. No one can match his teachings, his works, or his vicarious sacrifice. In addition, the fruits of Christianity—its benevolent works—far excel all others.

I also mentioned, Tim, that Christ is the only way to God. This means that we have an awesome privilege and responsibility to share the gospel. If we fail to carry the message to others, God in his mercy will judge them differently from us. For our Lord clearly taught that to whom much has been given, from him much shall be required. Since we have been privileged to know him and to have tasted of his goodness, God expects more of us than he does of those who have never heard the gospel. And since heaven and hell are realities, we must share the good news. It is criminal to withhold it.

May the Lord help us to be faithful witnesses. Take care. God be with you, Tim.

All my love,
Dad

A Christian Lifestyle

Dear Tim,

In the two final letters in this book let me share some of the qualities that I think should characterize a Christian's lifestyle.

First of all, as Christians we should be active *in* society—not withdraw from it. Unlike some religious leaders who are primarily concerned with escaping from this world into the next, Jesus' primary concern was to do the will of God in this world. His kind of religion included both the vertical relationship (love for God), and also the horizontal one (love for neighbor). The vertical relationship included not only solitary prayer, meditation, and communion with God, but also regular Sabbath worship in the synagogue (Mark 1:35; 6:46; Luke 4:16). The horizontal dimension of his worship not only included fellowship with disciples and friends, but also a ministry of redemption and liberation to those who were captive to sickness, sin, sorrow, and oppression (Luke 4:16-19).

Jesus associated closely with many men and women, but his inner circle of friends was composed of twelve men (Luke 8:1-3; 10:38-41; Mark 3:13-19; 16:1). From among these twelve disciples, Jesus chose three to be his intimate friends—Peter, James, and John. With his disciples he shared his innermost thoughts—his hopes and aspirations. They shared common values and goals, and for this reason his fellowship with them was especially meaningful and supportive.

He not only associated with close friends of like mind, but he moved in the mainstream of life where he encountered many with diverse points of view. He went where people were, where they were hurting and in need, as well as where they were rejoicing (Mark 1:29-34; John 2:1-11).

I'm pleased that you follow a similar pattern, Tim. You try to be faithful in your private devotional life, as well as in the worship, fellowship, and outreach ministry of the church. Your close friends—Dirk, Greg, Conrad—share your commitment to Christ. But you also have many friends with different religious perspectives, and some who are atheists and agnostics.

I once heard of a Christian (?) who boasted that "no non-Christian had ever been entertained in *his* home!" What a tragedy! How can one love and witness to his neighbor if he refuses to associate with him? As children of the light we are to illuminate Christ's way and to dispel the darkness (Matthew 5:14-16). And as salt we serve as a preservative and as seasoning within society (Matthew 5:13). We only truly find life when we are willing to lose it in service to others (Mark 8:35). It is self-contradictory for one to say that he loves God, while he refuses to relate to others (James 2:14-17; 1 John 4:20-21). It's really blasphemous. Or to put it another way, to profess faith verbally without active participation within society is "sound and fury, signifying nothing!"

Second, Tim, a Christian is not only a person who is actively involved in society, but also one who recognizes that his fellow Christians may differ in the ways they express their commitment. This is especially seen in the wide diversity of social practices condoned and condemned, modes of worship, and doctrines held by different churches and denominations. Honest, finite persons will differ. I'm thankful that you have the ability to empathize—to put yourself in another person's shoes—and see things from his perspective. Understanding the background and situations of others makes it easier to understand and relate to them.

Unfortunately, many Christians tend to think in absolute terms about many social practices that are not strictly forbidden in Scripture. They see things as either black or white, right or wrong, with no shades of gray. While all Christians acknowledge that there are absolutes, such as the Ten Commandments and the two Great Commandments, some want to establish all kinds of absolute rules for behavior (Exodus 20:1-17; Mark 12:28-33).

Some Christians legislate minor elements of social behavior, saying that one shouldn't do this or that or the other thing. Some even believe that one should only read the Bible—nothing else. And some claim that a college or university education is sinful! Actually, I imagine you could find a group of Christians who would condemn anything that you could name as sinful—especially if it were enjoyable! I think a good operating principle is this: if a belief or practice is not explicitly forbidden by Scripture, then Christians should be free to decide among themselves whether or not they wish to encourage a particular belief or practice. It's always helpful to seek the guidance of the Holy Spirit and the Word of God, as well as the counsel of mature Christian friends within the church, when making important choices and decisions.

Obviously, if something is injurious to oneself or others, it should be avoided. The apostle James observes that anyone "who knows the good he ought to do and doesn't do it, sins" (James 4:17). While he is speaking of the prompting of the Spirit to do something, it's equally valid to say that if the Spirit convicts us about a belief or practice we should carefully consider its worth and abandon or modify the belief or practice (1 Corinthians 8:1-13; 10:23).

Some practices may be right for one person, but not for another. Social standards—things considered right or wrong—vary, depending on one's denominational affiliation, socioeconomic background, level of education and knowledge, as well as one's racial and ethnic background. For example, most Lutherans, Roman Catholics, Episcopalians, Presbyterians, Methodists, and many Baptists believe social drinking is acceptable. But a minority within these denominations, as well as a majority within the smaller, more evangelical denominations and churches, believe that they should abstain from drinking alcoholic beverages. And they would label drinking a sin. Both groups use the Scriptures to justify their belief and practice.

While I don't drink alcoholic beverages, I must acknowledge that our Lord drank, that he turned water into real wine at the wedding at Cana of Galilee, and that the apostle Paul urged the young pastor, Timothy, to take some wine for his stomach ailment (Matthew 11:19; John 2:1-11; 1 Timothy 5:23). My decision not to drink, Tim, is not based on any prohibition of Scripture, but from my own religious conviction and experiences. I have noticed that excessive drinking causes a lot of ordinarily decent people to act foolishly and offensively—to put it mildly! I have never observed anyone whose behavior was improved by drinking. In addition, those driving while under the influence of alcohol have been responsible for the slaughter of hundreds of thousands of people on the highways. Nonetheless, I think that the decision to drink or not to drink rests with the individual. If one seeks God's guidance, he will give it.

Similarly, there are countless ways good Christians will differ from one another on social practices, doctrines, and modes of worship, as well as ways of witnessing by word and deed. We must respect one another's right to differ. While there is only one way to salvation, there are a variety of Christian lifestyles that are compatible with Scripture (Mark 9:38-39; Romans 14:5-23).

The important thing, Tim, is to stay close to Christ. Our Lord has promised not only to be with us, but also to reveal his will to us (Proverbs 3:5-6; Matthew 28:20; Luke 11:13; John 7:17; 14:16-17; 25-26; 15:26; 16:12-15). The important questions to ask concerning any practice are these: Will it make me a better Christian? Is it good for me, for my family, and for the church and community? Is it something that I would want everyone my age and sex to do? What will be the long run (not just the short run) consequences of my behavior?

Another important factor to consider is the influence our behavior has on others. The apostle Paul makes this point in his letter to the Corinthians. Some Christians had not fully broken with idolatry—they still harbored the idea that idols might have real power. So he said that even though mature Christians know that an idol is nothing, if a brother or sister believes that meat offered to an idol involves idol worship, out of consideration for the weaker brother or sister one should not eat it (1 Corinthians 8:1-13; 10:13—11:1). We all influence one another; make no mistake about that. I'm painfully aware of this fact when I observe some of my negative traits cropping up in one of you, my children.

Third, Tim, as a Christian you should develop your

abilities and gifts to their fullest extent. In your chosen position and career, give it all you've got so that both you and others will benefit. You, your brother, and sisters have taught me a great deal in this regard. In whatever you have engaged, you have all worked hard.

As you might expect, since I am involved in education, I believe that higher education is an invaluable aid to personal and professional development. It can help you acquire the skills you need to enter and advance in your chosen vocation. But more important, a good college or university education will provide breadth through its general education, the liberal arts core of required courses. The courses, reading, class interaction, as well as "bull sessions," all provide an opportunity to critically analyze and evaluate one's values and philosophy of life. While I wouldn't say that the "unexamined life is not worth living," it certainly is not the richest or most meaningful.

Because one's philosophy of life is so crucial, choose your college or university carefully. The advantage of attending a Christian institution is that the Christian philosophy of life is presented as a viable option, along with competing secular, religious, and philosophical systems. Many Christian professors teach in secular state and private colleges and universities. However, the values and philosophies propounded are often conflicting and hostile to theism or belief in God. In most secular institutions the Christian perspective is never presented as a legitimate philosophy of life.

Tim, sometimes special career interests necessitate attending a secular institution to secure the major or program desired. In these cases many attend a Christian college for one or two years because it provides an opportunity to take courses in the Christian faith, to think through one's beliefs, and to fellowship within a congenial, supportive environment. However, many Christians find the social interaction of the secular institution challenging. By participation in a campus Christian fellowship group and a church in the community, they not only "keep the faith," but grow in it.

So think things through carefully. Weigh the pros and cons of attending a Christian institution or a secular one. Consider both the long-run and the short-run advantages and disadvantages. One caution though, Tim. Don't let the cost be the determining factor. Financing can be arranged with combinations of loan, scholarship, and grant money. You go to college only once. Therefore, make your choice carefully and prayerfully on the basis of what you think is best for you.

Tim, you're probably saying, "Boy, I thought for sure you would say more than that about going to college!" I am— just a little. I couldn't pass up the opportunity. Your generation has advantages that many born earlier never had. Mom, for example, had to drop out of college after her sophomore year because she ran out of funds. If it were not for grants, loans, and scholarships, I probably never would have been able to go on to earn my college, seminary, and university degrees. ·

But today anyone with ability and demonstrated need can secure financial assistance. In addition, many students are able to work summers and part time during the college year. Your brother Steve said recently that the money he borrowed for his college education has paid for itself over and over again. In addition to his art, he secured a broad liberal arts education on which he is still building. I'm sure Susan and Debbi would agree, too. When you think of all the things people spend money for, such as cars that depreciate and are consumed, borrowing money for a college education is a wise investment. Earl Nightingale likened getting a college or university education to buying the goose that lays the golden egg. I heartily agree.

Nevertheless, I realize that college is not for everyone. Many choose to pursue careers that can be facilitated through apprenticeships and by attending a community college or a vocational school. One has to choose what he feels is best for him.

From a Christian perspective the important thing is that you choose a constructive vocation, one that will glorify God and benefit others, as well as yourself. I mean this in the broadest sense. Some well-meaning Christians rule out virtually all nonreligious careers, such as music and the performing arts. They seem to think that any performance or production that doesn't use religious terminology or doesn't attempt to "convert" people is worldly and sinful. As you might expect, Tim, I find this life negating, narrow, and un-Christian. All of the gifts God has given that enrich and deepen our appreciation and understanding of the wonder, mystery, and beauty of life are good.

However, I would draw the line at vocations or careers that demean, debase, cheapen, and exploit others. In addition to the obvious, such as running a porno shop, a gambling joint, or a house of prostitution, I would find it difficult working in large segments of the advertising industry. Madison Avenue creates desires in people for products they don't need and which are often physically and psychologically injurious. Nonmedicinal drugs, tobacco, liquor, certain foods, most of the cosmetic industry, and even parts of the clothing and appliance industry, are also hard to justify. The questions I think we should raise are these: Does my position involve responsible stewardship of human and natural resources? Will my work improve and enrich lives, or will it destroy them? When I come to the end of my life, can I meet the Lord and say without guilt, shame, or embarassment: "Lord, I've spent my life working/serving as a ___________________!"

Fourth, after having said that you should strive to be successful in your chosen vocation, Tim, a word is probably in order about the dangers of materialism. Jesus said: "No one can serve two masters; for either he will hate the one and love the other, or he will be devoted to the one and despise the other. You cannot serve God and mammon" (material wealth) (Matthew 6:24). The apostle Paul includes covetousness (greed) among such sins as immorality, impurity, passion, and evil desires (Colossians 3:5). He said that "the love of money is a root of all kinds of evil" (1 Timothy 6:6-10). Furthermore our Lord asks: "What good is it for a man to gain the whole world, yet forfeit his soul?" (Mark 8:36). He also reminds us that "a man's life does not consist in the abundance of his possessions" (Luke 12:15).

Tim, it occurred to me while in England last year that the new "opiate of the people" is materialism. It is the "drug" which has blinded our eyes, keeping us from seeing the true meaning of life (Mark 4:19; 10:17-25). The Marxist philosophy assumes that economic factors are basic to all others. I've alluded to it earlier. But what concerns me is that the United States and Canada, as well as other modern nations in the "free world," have succumbed to this opiate, or drug. We act as if life does consist of things, gadgets, and the pleasures of the flesh. I am not one to deny either the value of modern inventions that have made life easier or of legitimate pleasures, as you well know. But I believe that we have inverted our values and priorities. We attempt to find the meaning of life in the physical and material spheres, rather than finding the true meaning of life and the uses of material things within the context of our Christian experience

(Isaiah 55:1-3; Jeremiah 2:13; Luke 12:13-21; 15:11-32).

It's been my observation that those who make the acquisition of wealth and material things their goal have lost their souls in the process. There are others, however, who have become wealthy in the process of legitimately pursuing their careers or professions and by serving others. And of course, many, many more see love for God and love for neighbor as the supreme or highest good. Pursuing this latter course doesn't rule out acquiring wealth, but it views material resources as a trust from God to be used to minister to the needs of others (Luke 10:25-37; 19:1-10; Ephesians 4:28).

The parable of the rich farmer serves as a good illustration of the folly of making the pursuit of wealth one's goal in life (Luke 12:13-21; see also Luke 16:19-31; 18:18-30). Discontented with a good living, he became greedy, deciding to postpone enjoying life "today." He felt that after he made his fortune, then he could retire to a leisurely comfortable life. But he never did. He died "prematurely"—as we usually do! He never took the time to develop a meaningful relationship with his family and others about him. As a result, when he died his children, who had acquired their father's avaricious philosophy of life, fought among themselves for his wealth.

The truth is, Tim, that once we have made an idol of wealth, it's difficult to stop worshiping it. That is why the first commandment says, "You shall have no other gods before me" (Exodus 20:3). And that is why our Lord commanded us to "seek first his kingdom and his righteousness" (Matthew 6:33). If we accept the challenge, then all worthwhile things in life will come along, also.

So, Tim, strive to keep Christ first in your life. Let the Holy Spirit guide you. This won't mean that life will necessarily be easy—free from sickness, crises, problems, or even tragedy. For this is the common experience of all—Christian and non-Christian. But through faith in God you'll triumph and find "that in all things God works for the good of those who love him" (Romans 8:28; also see Romans 31:39; John 16:33; 1 Corinthians 10:13). There inevitably will be things that we'll not understand, for we can only partially know and understand in this life. But in the life to come, we will fully understand (1 Corinthians 13:12; 2 Corinthians 5:7; 1 John 3:1-3).

Tim, let me tie things together at this point. Draw near to Christ and he will give you the power of his Spirit to make your life count for him as you pursue your chosen career. Remember, Tim, your primary vocation is to be a Christian. Work with other Christians of like mind. Pray for them, as well as for others who follow a Christian lifestyle different from yours. Take advantage of every opportunity to increase your knowledge. As much as possible, Tim, beware of mammon—materialism. We cannot serve two masters. Therefore, guard against all that would dethrone Christ as Lord of your life.

I'll stop here, Tim. I'll finish up in my next letter. I hope you're enjoying your work at the hotel in Ocean City. Be careful when surfing and kayaking in the ocean. While I am not up to those sports, I hope to spend some time on the beach with you when mom and I come down.

God be with you. Hope to see you soon.

I love you, Tim
Dad

Letter **18**

The Importance
of Love

Dear Tim,

In my previous letter I mentioned four characteristics that should be inherent in a Christian lifestyle. In this final letter, let me mention several more.

The first quality that I want to mention is love. Just as the primary attribute of God is love, so Christians should be motivated by love in all their relationships with others (1 John 4:7-21). John teaches us that we derive our capacity to love from God, and then our love flows out to God, others, and to ourselves—in that order. Our Lord said: "Whoever comes to me cannot be my disciple unless he loves me more than his father and his mother, his wife and his children, his brothers and his sisters, and himself as well" (Luke 14:26, TEV). This is difficult for some Christians to understand and accept, but it really makes good sense to me. Let me tell you why.

When Jesus was asked, "Which commandment is the most important of all?" he replied, "The most important one is this: 'Listen, Israel! The Lord our God is the only Lord. Love the Lord your God with all your heart, with all your soul, with all your mind, and with all your strength.' The second most important commandment is this: 'Love your neighbor as you love yourself' " (Mark 12:28-31, TEV). Both the vertical God-man relationship and the horizontal man-man relationship are essential to a healthy Christian life. And the vertical must come before the horizontal relationship.

It is only through the proper worship of God that we can bring our lives into harmony with his will for us, and have the kind of relationships with others that we should. Micah, the Old Testament prophet, said, "The Lord has told us what is good. What he requires of us is this: to do what is just, to show constant love, and to live in humble fellowship with our God" (6:8, TEV). Just by using this brief prophetic statement, Tim, we can examine our lives by asking: Have I been just and loving in my relationships with God, with my parents, with my wife or husband, with my brothers and sisters, with others, and with myself? Have I walked humbly with God? Or have I tried to usurp his role by playing God? Have I been humble before God, as well as in my relations with others?

Once the vertical relationship between God and us is cleared of all obstructions, once we have humbly submitted to God's Word and Spirit and gained or regained a proper perspective, then we can have the kind of horizontal relationships that are pleasing to God. In fact, John insists that our love for God can only be authenticated by sincere, caring relationships with others (1 John 3:10, 14:18; 4:20-21; compare 1:5-7). Therefore, honest and open communication with God and submission to his will should naturally result in positive and fulfilling relationships with family and others. Fulfilling the "first" commandment properly will inevitably lead to fulfilling the "second."

I would liken the relationship between an individual and God, as well as those between individuals, to the rela-

188

tionships among the sides of an equilateral triangle. In the case of the Christian, the triangle is resting on one side. The base symbolizes God, the foundation. The sides represent self and others who, when properly rooted in God, have harmonious relationships. This is symbolized by the two lines coming together at the apex, or top. Sickness, problems, disappointments, tragedy, and death of loved ones will come to us as they come to all. The Christian is not exempt from these; but the God in whom we trust will sustain us in times of trial and testing. Since we are rooted in God, we experience a peace and security those outside of Christ never know. While we may be shaken to the very foundation, we will not fail. He will hold us fast (Matthew 7:24-25; Luke 22:31-32; Hebrews 6:19-20; 13:5b-6; Isaiah 43:2-3a; Psalms 23 and 46).

Individuals who are not rooted in God are often like an equilateral triangle precariously balancing on an apex. They are not only toppled by the trials and testings that come along, but the relationships between them and others are not harmonious. This is symbolized by the distance between the two vertical lines that diverge from the apex base (Matthew 7:26-27; Isaiah 57:20-21; James 4:1-6; 1 John 3:11-12).

Another important point about love is this. We don't have the option of being a loving person or not being a loving person. As Christians we have been commanded by our Lord to love (John 15:12; Mark 12:31-32). Furthermore, the love he calls for is a special love. It is a God-like kind of love: agape is the word used in the Greek New Testament. It is a caring love that shows itself in attitudes and actions. It's the kind of love that continues when ordinary love runs out or quits. When the other person is unkind, unfeeling, and unresponsive, it keeps on loving. It's the kind of love that God demonstrated for us in Christ when we were rebellious, unresponsive, and disobedient to him (Romans 5:8).

Tim, let me make just one more point about love. Love is not an emotion, as many believe. Love involves the emotions, but is primarily an attitude, a disposition to act in a caring, responsible manner. It should not be confused with the kind of sentimentality that condones clearly unethical behavior by falsely labeling it "love."

I might add here, and not in passing, that justice is a part of love. It is really the other side of the coin. I've thought a great deal about this lately. Christ not only perfectly embodied love, but he also embodied justice. He opposed those who were hypocritical and unjust (Matthew 23:1-39; also see the parables of Jesus—many of them have justice as their theme). He didn't remain silent in the presence of unjust and exploitive behavior. That wouldn't have been good for the oppressed or the oppressor in the long or the short run. Our Lord also expects us to oppose evil when we encounter it. We're not to fear the wicked who might destroy our bodies, but fear God who might reject us for failing to take a stand for justice (Matthew 10:26-31).

Second, while we are thinking about love, let me say that another characteristic of a Christian lifestyle is marrying within the faith. As an instructor of sociology specializing in family sociology, you probably knew that I would bring this up sooner or later! But really, they are related.

As Christians we can worship and serve God best by marrying someone who shares a similar commitment to God in Christ. When both husband and wife have agreed that the vertical relationship with God takes priority, then the horizontal relationships between them can be maximized, or be at their best. Only then can they create the kind of home life in which the faith of parents, children, and friends are fed and nurtured. Our Lord promised that "where two or three come together in my name," he would be there to bless (Matthew 18:20). The family ought to be such a place.

A Christian mate is essential. Before you get involved with a particular young woman, however, it would be helpful if you identified the qualities you'd like to have in a wife and mother of your children. Be realistic, yet flexible, because no one can ever fully measure up to the ideal. While you're compiling your "requirements," keep in mind that young women are identifying the qualities that they would like to have in a husband. So continue to develop those character traits you already have that make for meaningful, edifying, and enriching interpersonal relationships, and acquire others you feel you lack. Incidentally, the same qualities that facilitate communication while you are single will also contribute to a happy, workable marriage.

I might emphasize, Tim, that while intelligent, mature, committed Christians have a better chance at happiness in marriage than non-Christians, this doesn't mean that the Christian's marriage will be free of conflict and stress. Conflict and problems are an integral part of marriage, just as they are an integral part of the single person's life. There's nothing wrong with conflict and problems, if they are negotiated and resolved. If we use them as opportunities to grow through compromise, adaptation, or accommodation, then they have served a useful purpose. The Christian couple has the advantage of having agreed upon a basic set of ground rules for a good working marriage relationship— the teachings and principles of our Lord. By accepting one of Christ's basic concepts, that of mutual servanthood, and by following other principles which he set forth, the oneness sought in marriage can be realized (Mark 10:42-45; Ephesians 5:21; Philippians 2:3).

Occasionally you'll meet a married couple who claim that

they never have had conflict in their marriage. I met an older couple like that when I served a church in North Carolina. The man who made that claim also said that he had never apologized to anyone! Obviously, his wife was not permitted any expression at all. (If he wanted her opinion, he gave it to her.) Within a marriage, as within a friendship, there must be release, the freedom to be oneself—to express one's own opinion without being "put down" or ridiculed. Only within an open relationship characterized by mutual respect and trust, where constructive conflict is welcomed, can there be wholesome growth and development.

Tim, let me just say a few words about the place of physical intimacy within dating and courtship. On the whole, I think that this is best played down or minimized. I say this because the physical display of affection comes naturally, in both a *positive* and a *negative* sense. Positively, if a couple is serious about each other, they should first test for compatibility in other areas than the physical—such as values, goals, interests, hobbies, philosophy of life, and husband/father, wife/mother role definitions. After you have had time to explore these things, then the display of affection will come naturally, because a sense of mutuality and caring has developed. If the physical comes first, it supplants the time that should be given to exploring the non-physical areas where compatibility is needed. Physical involvement has a way of narrowing the field of perception, often blinding a couple to significant areas of difference.

Negatively, young people ought to be on guard because biological drives seek satisfaction and have a way of "taking over." Physical attraction to the opposite sex does not necessarily mean "love" at all. Probably, it merely means that one has a physical desire for sexual intimacy with a member of the opposite sex (2 Samuel 13:1-17).

Dr. Joseph Faulkner, a Penn State University sociologist, put it pretty well when he said that a want does not constitute a need. We want a lot of things—cars, stereos, and sex. But we don't really need them. We can live without a car, without a stereo. And we can live without sex, although you would never think so when you read the newspapers and magazines or view TV and movies. Countless men and women down through the centuries have exercised self-control and entered marriage as virgins. A great many have remained faithful within marriage, too. And many have lived the single life without sex.

Dr. Faulkner didn't say that it is easy to exercise self-control. It isn't. But if one has made up his mind that he will wait until marriage to participate in sex, exercising self-control is a great deal easier. Self-control is the Christian ideal and it is within our capabilities. When our biological desires are controlled until we find someone to whom we're ready to make a formal, legal commitment, and with whom we wish to establish a Christian home, then the physical union brings the joy we seek and the joy God intended.

So, Tim, take your time. You've mentioned a lot of things you'd like to do before you marry. There's no reason to rush into it. Try not to get too involved with a girl until you have accomplished the goals you've set for yourself. When you're ready to settle down, find a good Christian girl, and have a reasonably long courtship. Get to know her, her family, and her friends well. Contrary to what many young people believe, you do marry the family. Also, you marry the family in the sense that you will interact with her parents. They will be your in-laws. Furthermore, Tim, children have a way of acquiring the behavior patterns of their parents. While I recognize that we are unique individuals in our own right, this ought not to blind us to environmental and hereditary factors within the family of a prospective wife.

Make certain that you both like each other. Commit yourselves to each other with that special agape love. It's the kind of love that will carry you over the rough spots. It will see you through the inevitable plateaus or "sahara" periods in marriage.

Third, in addition to love, a good Christian and a good happy home must have a sense of discipline. Tim, I want to commend you for your sense of discipline, not only the rigorous physical discipline you put yourself through for skiing, but the orderliness with which you live your life. I like the way you keep things in proper perspective—the way you use your Christian values to guide you in your choices and decision making. I'm sure that your values are reinforced and strengthened by your devotional life and involvement in the church.

Since you're into sports, you can appreciate the analogy Paul uses when writing of discipline. Writing about a race he said: "Surely you know that many runners take part in a race, but only one of them wins the prize. Run, then, in such a way as to win the prize. Every athlete in training submits to strict discipline, in order to be crowned with a wreath that will not last; but we do it for one that will last forever. That is why I run straight for the finish line..." (1 Corinthians 9:24-26a, TEV). As Christians we ought to keep before us one goal, that of loving God and neighbor. We ought also to maintain the discipline faithfully ourselves, not just "preach" to others. Unless we keep the rules ourselves, Paul says that we ourselves may be disqualified from the race (1 Corinthians 9:27).

Interestingly enough, Tim, to modify his analogy a bit, as Christians we are not necessarily concerned about coming in first; although we should strive to do our best. Our primary concern should be faithfulness and finishing the race (1 Corinthians 4:2; 2 Timothy 4:7-8). Someone asked Mother Teresa of Calcutta if she didn't get discouraged with her work with the destitute and dying. She replied, "God has not called me to be successful. He has called me to be faithful." From the world's perspective she may be a loser—spending her life with the sick and dying, but from our Lord's perspective she's a winner. The last (the servant) shall be first. Those who finish first from the world's perspective, who use power and authority to control and manipulate others to their own advantage, shall be last (Mark 10:41-45).

Fourth, Tim, in addition to living a well-disciplined life, the Christian should be one who is accepting of others. We should try, as much as we can, to be kind and gracious in our relationships with others (Romans 12:9-21; Ephesians 4:17-32; Philippians 4:4a, 8-9). I want to encourage you to continue to develop a kind and gracious disposition. Ever since childhood you have been a caring and sharing person. I'm pleased that you have always related well to persons of all ages—children, adults, and older people. I remember the surprised response of our neighbor in Nottingham, England, when you took time to visit with her. She remarked how rare it is for young people to take time to visit with an older person.

Sometimes you'll meet some formally educated people—college and university, as well as business and professional people—who think they're "a cut above" the common man. Sometimes people who are less advantaged think that those whom they view as rich are snobbish. The old often pass up the young, or the young ignore the old. Often racial and ethnic groups are blinded by prejudice and discriminate against one another. But we all—rich, poor, educated, un-educated, racial and ethnic groups, female and male, handicapped and unhandicapped—make up the body of Christ. Everyone and each group has strengths and weaknesses, virtues and vices—but we need each other! When we neglect or slight one part of the body, all suffer. We all lose.

Finally, Tim, strengthen your positive attitude of gratitude, of giving thanks to God for his goodness (Philippians 4:4-8; Ephesians 5:20). I have never met a grateful Christian who was habitually cynical, sarcastic, or soured on life. Grateful people are usually optimistic, positive, and productive. Habitual ingratitude not only turns one into a whiner, a complainer, and a fault finder, but also makes one unpleasant to be around. An attitude of gratitude sustains us during the dry, hard times through which all of us must inevitably pass.

By way of summary then, the essence of Christianity is love. Being a loving person is not an option. It is our Lord's command. When we love him first, then we can properly love our neighbor as we love ourselves. Love is a caring attitude—the fruit of God's indwelling Spirit. The more we pattern our lives after Christ's, the more loving we become. If your home is to be a place where love dwells, marry in the faith, so your family will be a Christian one in which each member can grow in Christ and serve him.

In addition to love, discipline is another mark of a Christian lifestyle. Discipline should include regular personal and corporate worship and service. And finally, I mention that as Christians we should accept others where they are and try to give them support, in so far as they are pursuing a righteous path.

So, then, Tim, continue your positive attitude toward others. Continue to give thanks to God for all things. And yes, Tim, even give thanks for the difficult experiences that provide you with an opportunity to exercise your faith and thereby come to know the boundless grace of God in Christ that sustains and strengthens both of us.

May the Lord continue to lead and guide you throughout all your days.

I love you, Tim, my son,
Dad

An Afterword of Thanks

I wish to express my gratitude to my wife, Norma, and to our children, Steve, Debbi, Susan, and Tim. Through the give and take within our family we have all been able to share and grow in the faith. Their love, understanding, and patience with a husband and a father such as I have enabled them to develop the three above virtues. I have given them all-too-many opportunities to exercise these virtues.

Before I wrote the final draft of the letters in this book, I asked a number of friends if they would read the manuscript and give me some feedback. They did—and I'm indebted to them for it: Hugh Williamson (Methodist, dean of arts and sciences at Lock Haven State College), John Plank (American Baptist, elementary school science teacher), Charles Mason (Episcopalian priest), Gene and Bea Heid (Evangelical, physician and homemaker), Alice Miller (United Presbyterian elder), Bob McLaughlin (Baptist General Conference, minister), Gerald Cierpilowski (Roman Catholic, professor of education), Neil Turner (United Presbyterian, college wrestling coach), and Bill Smith-Hinds (United Brethren in Christ, associate professor of sociology, and minister).

Of course, my son Tim, who requested the letters, was the first to read them, and I especially appreciated his response and concerns. My wife, Norma, helped by her meticulous proofreading and grammatical suggestions. Steve and Nadine, Tim's older brother and sister-in-law, also read the letters carefully and offered constructive suggestions. Donna Barton and Ann Peter assisted by deciphering my writing and typing the manuscript.

A couple of words of special thanks are due. One to John and Sandra Drescher, authors of a father-daughter book of their own, for writing a fine introduction to *Dear Tim*. A second word of special thanks is due Paul M. Schrock, book editor at Herald Press, for his assistance all along the way. His willingness to share his theological knowledge and editorial skills enabled me to get the letters ready for press.

Charles P. De Santo is an ordained Presbyterian minister and has long been actively involved in the life of the church. He has served as regular and supply minister in churches in North Carolina, Indiana, Tennessee, Kansas, Kentucky, and Pennsylvania. He is a frequent guest speaker to church and college youth groups on the theme of courtship and marriage. His book, *Love and Sex Are Not Enough*, continues to be popular among young people.

Married to the former Norma A. Michener, they are the parents of four children: Steve, Debbi, and Susan who are all married, and Tim, who pops in and out of the homestead in Mackeyville, Pennsylvania. Tim thrives on tennis, kayaking, and skiing—skiing being his first love. Tim is training at Pats Peak Academy, Henniker, New Hampshire, where he competes in downhill and slalom races. During the fall semester, Tim attends college.

De Santo is presently professor of sociology and chairman of the department of sociology/anthropology/and social work at Lock Haven State College, Lock Haven, Pennsylvania. After attending Houghton College and Temple University (BS 1949), he earned the MDiv from Louisville Presbyterian Theological Seminary (1952) and the PhD in biblical studies from Duke University (1957). He taught biblical studies, philosophy of religion, and theology at Maryville College (Tenn.) and Sterling College (Kan.), also serving as dean of the chapel at the later institution. For a year he taught Hebrew and Old Testament at Wheaton College (Ill.) He earned his MA in sociology from Ball State University (1968). Prior to his present position which he has held since 1969, De Santo taught sociology and religion at Huntington College (Ind.) He served as an exchange professor at Trent Polytechnic, Nottingham, England, in 1972-73, and more recently in 1978-79—when he began to write his letters on basic Christian beliefs to his son.

In addition to *Dear Tim* and *Love and Sex Are Not Enough*, De Santo is author of a *Commentary on the Book of Revelation* (Baker, 1967) and editor of *A Reader in Sociology: Christian Perspectives* (Herald Press, 1980). His articles have appeared in *Eternity, Christianity Today, Religion in Life*, and other Christian periodicals.

Tim with his mother, Norma De Santo

My wife, Norma, and I have been blessed with four fine children—each unique in his or her own way. (Unbiased reporting, of course!) Through tough times and good times we have worked things out together.

While I have addressed these letters to Tim, my youngest son, in reality I'm sharing them with my other children as well—Steve, Debbi, and Susan. I hope the letters will stimulate their thinking about basic Christian beliefs and also serve as a means of Christian growth.

I'm glad that many other young people will look over Tim's shoulder and read these letters also. If you have already given your life to the Lord, I hope that the letters will help you grow in your faith. If you have not, I pray that reading the letters with an open mind will nudge you toward embracing Christ as your own Savior and the Lord of your life.

—*Charles P. De Santo*

Cover photo by Stock Photos Unlimited, New York

ISBN 0-8361-1991